HOW TO CONDUCT

Spiritual Warfare

MARY GARRISON

WHITAKER
HOUSE

How to Conduct Spiritual Warfare

ISBN: 978-1-62911-017-2
eBook ISBN: 978-1-62911-041-7
Printed in the United States of America
© 1980, 2014 by Mary Garrison

Whitaker House
1030 Hunt Valley Circle
New Kensington, PA 15068
www.whitakerhouse.com

1 2 3 4 5 6 7 8 9 10 11 ᲚᲘᲚ 21 20 19 18 17 16 15 14

CONTENTS

PREFACE

Have you wondered why so many of God's servants lately are becoming writers? Have you noticed that many of them are writing books on demons and what to do about them, which is often called "spiritual warfare"? Indeed, God has compelled many of us who have been trained by the Holy Spirit to inform Christ followers that they can overcome Satan and his evil ones and win victories for God.

Don't be deceived by those who won't listen to what the Spirit says to the church today. If there were only a few proclaiming this truth, we could assume it was unimportant. But the sound of the trumpet of Zion has sounded for thousands to pick up their arms and engage in spiritual warfare.

Yes, there is a great stirring in the household of God this day. You need only to look on the shelves of Christian bookstores or tune in to religious radio stations to confirm this truth. You will hear ministers of God trying to get the message across, and there is great need for this communication, for the devil and his false prophets have declared war upon the saints, and he will prevail against them if they are not ready.

God, as I see it, has begun preparing His followers. He is raising up a mighty army that will go forth in overcoming power, winning blood–bought victories for Christ. The only way Satan and his demons can take the kingdom is by force; they will not give up the souls of men without a fight.

Now, as I see it, no one writer or preacher reveals everything God wants us to know. But each writer has something important to contribute to our knowledge of spiritual warfare, which is why God has told many of His servants to write.

We must learn how to try the spirits so that we can "eat the meat and spit out the bones." When God told me to write *How to Try a Spirit*, He showed me that while I was reaching hundreds by ministering and speaking, I could reach thousands more by writing. He promised protection for the disciples who prepare fellow Christians for that terrible, painful time that is ahead.

Those who ignore this mighty spiritual battle will miss out on the rewards promised by Jesus to those who overcome. (See Revelation 2:7, 11, 17, 26–28; 3:5, 12, 21; 21:7.) Do you want to miss out on them? Not me!

The Prophecy

A prophecy was spoken during a 1975 conference on Pentecost. It is a word we still need to hear and obey this very hour. This word from God should be shared with all of God's family. This conviction causes me to make a closer analysis of this prophecy and share my interpretation with you. Let us first take a look at the prophecy:

I speak to you of the dawn of a new age for My church. I speak to you of a day that has not yet been seen before.... Prepare yourselves for the action that I begin now, because things that you see around you will change. The combat that you will engage in is different and new. You need wisdom from Me that you do not yet have. You need the power of My Holy Spirit in a way that you have not yet possessed it. You need an understanding of My will and My ways that you do not yet contain. Open your eyes and your hearts to receive Me and the day that I have set in motion.

Here is what we can glean from this prophetic word:

1. "Prepare yourselves." God did not say to wait on Him to prepare you. No, He said, "Train *yourself* for the way—for action!" When? Now. Why? There is a battle to fight. How? It is to be a spiritual battle. We do not wrestle flesh and blood but principalities of the air. (See Ephesians 6:12.) The Bible states that God will not do anything without first telling His servants. (See Amos 3:7.) Therefore, He is revealing warfare tactics through the enlightenment of His prophets. But it is not enough to listen to the prophets, we must also act on what they say.

2. "You need wisdom from Me that you do not yet have. You need the power of My Holy Spirit in a way that you have not yet possessed it. You need an understanding of My will and My ways that you do not yet contain." He said that you need more knowledge about this new battle you will now enter into. You need to know who you will battle—their names, methods of warfare, and reasons for fighting. Down through the

ages, God has used man, inspired by the Holy Spirit, to speak to His people. The meaning of the Scriptures has been revealed to them; they have been allowed to see the truth that is needed to overcome the enemy. For many years, God has been preparing them to equip His people. "Well, then," you may ask, "what is the problem?"

3. "Open your eyes and your hearts to receive Me and the day that I have set in motion." God has been giving us information on things to come and strict instructions on what to do. But many leaders have allowed Satan to blind them, and keep them blinded, to this great spiritual battle. Many of the people under them are being affected by this new battle and have not been properly prepared to fight.

    However, this message is not just for leaders but for the followers. Many of God's seasoned servants have been given certain truths, and they have shared these truths with their followers. God has commanded them to write books on the information, instructions, and knowledge revealed to them, and through prayer and fasting, they have trained God's people. But the people's eyes and hearts were closed, and many of them rejected the words of the prophets.

My books are only a small part of God's preparation plan. They take the veil off of Satan and his strongmen, revealing their true names and fruits, and how to resist them. When we shine the spotlight upon the dark forces, we can then overcome them until the end.

The Bible says the gates of hell cannot prevail against the church. (See Matthew 16:18.) That is to say, the gates of hell are not strong enough to resist a direct attack, or onslaught, of the church. Some people are of the opinion that when the gates of hell start pushing and assaulting the gates of the church, they don't have to fight back; they are safe within the walls. But this is a reversal of what God intends for us. Why did He give us the armor of God and the sword of power and the great weapons of warfare, mighty through God to pull down strongholds? To keep peace with Satan and his demons? I should say not! He gave them to us to fight, to storm the gates of hell, and to put the devil to flight! So, get off your pews, church, and start invading, persuading, and prevailing!

ONE

QUEST FOR SPIRITUAL REALITIES

Man instinctively desires to know the unknown. He knows that there is much more than what meets the natural eye. He has seen supernatural manifestations, healings, and other amazing phenomenon. One can hardly pick up a newspaper, turn on a television, or visit a bookstore without seeing some reference to the supernatural.

For years, I have observed a growing interest in many people to know more about the spirit world. They look at a dead body, realize the person is no longer there, and wonder where the spirit goes.

I believe that most human beings are intensely interested in "unseen" things. Just look at the growing sales of occult literature. I have read that many writers are zeroing in on this market. One author of many such books stated that she was neither a psychic nor a medium but that she wrote for the money, because of the sales of similar books.

People are turning to lies because mature Christians are not publishing the truths, which are far more exciting. Multitudes are searching for the truth that many mature Christians are holding in! My heart breaks at the thought. These people are after the gospel truth that we are supposed to be shouting from the rooftops!

They are indeed on a quest for new spiritual realities. Most of the time, the first people they consult are church members and ministers. You may not realize it, but ask those who have turned to the occult for answers, and you will find that this is true. Occult leaders give them the "truth" they are looking for, which is more than they received from us.

God gave the church the gifts to equip and perfect the saints in every good work. (See Ephesians 4:12.) The church is supposed to meet all of the spiritual needs of the seekers. Yet when many seekers come to us for help, we refer them to psychiatrists, physicians, etc. Finding no help or answers from them, they may seek the wisdom of one with a familiar spirit—a medium or witch. Brethren, this should not be! God has given us spiritual wisdom, revelation knowledge, gifts, and truth. We have all of the keys to the kingdom.

I do not believe that God is pleased with the cop-out of His church! Only knowing the truth will set people free! And all the truth we shall ever need is contained in the precious Book that Christians carry around.

Fear of public opinion keeps many ministers from educating themselves on the deliverance of the oppressed. They do not want to lose the esteem of their peers. Shouldn't we be more concerned with pleasing the One who chose us to soldier for Him? Look at the example of deliverance ministry Christ gave to us. If you follow in His example, regardless of the consequences, you will surely please Him!

If you search for answers to your questions about the spiritual world, under the guidance of the Holy Ghost, you will discover more exciting truths about spiritual beings, death, the afterlife, spiritual warfare, spiritual gifts, supernatural powers, and so on, than you ever dreamed possible.

I have found that there is no end to my adventure in the spiritual realm. When I seek, I find. When I knock, He answers. I can go as fast and as far as I am ready to go in exploring God's truths. If God knows, I can know. He does not upbraid me when I ask Him; He answers my questions. After all, I'm being conformed into the likeness of His Son.

If someone comes to me and asks me to help them, I can say, "Of course. You have surely come to the right place. I can do all things through Christ who strengthens me. The kingdom of God is at hand. If Jesus says His kingdom is within me, then it's there. What do you want from God?" That is bold! This is what we need—holy boldness.

If they ask a medium for help, what do you think he or she will say? "I'm sorry, my dear, we should not delve into those things. We might get into error as some of those far-out Christians are!" I should say not! She will give them satanic knowledge!

Aren't we supposed to have power and knowledge that exceeds that of Satan's realm? Then, what is the problem? Why have we failed?

The moment a mature Christian publishes or preaches God's truths, all hell breaks loose. The devil himself stirs up many ministers to come against him or her. These satanic helpers drop little hints, comments, and lies that stir up strife. Here is Satan's strategy:

1. Kill his influence
2. Discredit him
3. Cut him off at the onset

Satan doesn't dare set witches against Christians. Then they would recognize the enemy and fight him. No, he uses the brethren who do not know a demon from an angel and are too haughty to learn the truth.

The saints shall overcome Satan with the word of their testimony and the blood of Jesus. We must not love our lives but lay them down for Him. (See Revelation 12:11.) Are we so concerned with our lives, reputations, and careers that we are losing the battle? Without confrontation, there is no victory. Confront the evil forces working in your life. You can walk in Christ's victory!

TWO

THE GIFT OF
DISCERNING OF SPIRITS

"Lord, I pray thee, open his eyes, that he may see."
—2 Kings 6:17

The gift of discerning of spirits is hard to describe, but I think there is a great need for us to try. When I received the gift, it felt as if I had been spiritually blind and suddenly received my sight. It enabled me to serve God in a far greater capacity. Now when I minister, I can see problems and react properly to them.

This gift opened me up to the supernatural realm. I could see with "spirit eyes" exactly what was happening in the unseen world—the evil spirits and their crafty tricks and devices. I could decipher their motives. I could even see the leadings of the Holy Spirit—how He wanted to use me, and what He wished to accomplish in any given situation, to bring about God's purposes.

At these times, I observe everything going on in the room. I can see needs in people that God desires to meet, and how the evil spirits use not only sinners but also saints to stop these needs from being met. In the past, I've observed seasoned ministers lend themselves to Satan's work, or unknowingly block the work of the Holy Spirit by changing the subject when a seeker inquires of the truth. We must realize that both God and Satan use people to accomplish their wills. We are a servant to whomever we yield our devotion!

The discerning of spirits also shows which gifts of the Holy Spirit are manifesting in a church service. The person with the gift of discernment can see how God is working and how evil spirits are working. If the saints realized the importance of the gift of discerning of spirits and allowed it to operate in the church, they would be able to accomplish so much more for Christ. It would be safer in that there would not be as many perverse, false spirits leading our congregations.

Discerning of spirits allows a person to judge the gifts to know if they are genuine. This judgment should not be left to the person who does not understand spiritual things and fights God's power and gifts. Yet there are so many novices in charge? When God builds the church, the gates of hell will not prevail against it. Why? The gifts God gave us are His own powers! Jesus ascended on high and gave gifts to men that are far superior to anything we or Satan can muster up.

The gift of discerning of spirits cannot be compared to man's ability to discern, imagine, or make an educated guess about a person's thought life or motivations. Discerning *people* is not even the purpose of this gift; the purpose is to allow the believer to discern the spirits by name.

What spirits are at work? Is it God? The Holy Spirit? An angel? A demon? Satan himself? A good, ministering spirit? A familiar spirit? If evil spirits are present, what are they doing? If they are there, you better believe they are up to something. They have a plan and will successfully execute that plan if they are not resisted. Saints, this is important to know! Evil forces use their power to breed evil; this evil stands until a stronger power overpowers it. Can you see why we cannot be idle during this war? We need to be undoing heavy burdens, loosing bands of wickedness, breaking human curses, and freeing the oppressed!

When Elisha was describing the way the battle was lining up to his servant, he counted more spirits to help them than soldiers to come against them. (See 2 Kings 6:17.) He saw the armies of God! When the gift of discerning of spirits is in operation, we, too, can see the battle raging over the souls of men. It is as if the course of the battle depends on the way we fight. The believer can command both sides. The Bible says that the spirits are subject to *us*! (See Luke 10:20.) What an awesome responsibility! It's true that we have power over their power, but we must use it.

The powerful gift of discerning of spirits incorporates the gifts and attributes of God to give the worker a "God's-eye view" of all situations. When I am using that gift in my ministry, I am no longer operating on man's level, with his knowledge and power, but on God's level, with divine knowledge and sight. Nothing is withheld from me. If I am counseling someone, I see their need from beginning to end. Usually, this revelation has no relation to what they are telling me at the time. It is as if their lives become transparent to me, and I can "discern" them, knowing all the things God wants me to see and act on. He never reveals private and personal matters that are none of my business, except when He wishes to expose them. God reveals only what is for their good.

We do not operate the gift of discernment; the Holy Spirit in us is in charge of it. He decides how, when, and where it is used. We can try the spirits by their fruits, but this divine gift carries us far beyond all of that! It is given to perfect the saints, to prepare them for God. Therefore, God is the only One who can lift the veil on falsehood. The Holy Spirit leads and guides us into all truth!

THREE

HOW TO
TRY A SPIRIT

It is important that everyone knows how to try a spirit by its fruit. Trying the spirits has been of the utmost importance in the ministry. Christians need more insight in this field, and I have a holy unction from God to convey and reveal the knowledge I have on how to try a spirit to as many people as possible. The Holy Spirit has confirmed this call by giving me divine assistance beyond what I could have imagined.

I have not always known how to try a spirit. In fact, I didn't receive this gift until I received the gift of discerning of spirits. Before I learned how to try spirits, I was deceived many times. I suffered much because I had never heard anyone teach on the subject and did not know how to try a spirit. When I asked ministers about the spirits, how to know them and how to try them, some of them gave me some Scriptures but didn't really tell me much else. Although some did tell me to try a spirit by its fruit, they offered no insight as to what fruit belonged to which spirit.

Therefore, I was deceived many times, without realizing it. I also fell into a few satanic entrapments because of this lack of knowledge. The Holy Spirit always brought me out of these snares by teaching me the truth, thank God. But most of these experiences could have easily been avoided had I known more about spirits.

A Wolf in Sheepskin

The Bible tells us that in these last days, God's elect people will be deceived by Satan. This is easy for Satan to do if we disobey the Word and believe that every spirit that comes to us is of God.

Let us review what Jesus said in Matthew 7:15–16:

> *Beware of false prophets, which come to you in sheep's clothing, but inwardly they are ravening wolves. Ye shall know them by their fruits.*

These Scriptures contain the key to knowing spirits. We cannot improve the parable which Jesus used to teach us about evil spirits and their fruit; so let us look at it literally for a moment. Here are the truths we can glean:

1. Wolves cannot produce the same fruit as sheep.

2. They cannot grow wool.

3. They do not make good food for the table.

4. They cannot follow the shepherd obediently like sheep but mosey around sniffing.

5. Even though they have sheepskin, they do not feed upon the grass as sheep but, when they are hungry, they will eat the sheep.

6. They "fleece" the sheep.

The *"ravening wolves,"* or evil spirits, may fool you for a while, but they only produce fruit of their kind. Jesus said so, and He is the authority. He wants to tell us about all of these things, if we will just listen to Him!

A hunter knows that each animal will produce fruit of its own kind. He can decipher the kind of animal by its tracks and signs. No matter how well sheepskin covers a wolf, his tracks will give him away. The wolf might try to bleat like a sheep, but when he is alone, he will howl like the wolf that he is. Likewise, when you look at a citrus tree, you may not know whether it is an orange, tangerine, lemon, lime, grapefruit, or kumquat tree at first glance, but you *will* know when you see its fruit. So it is with evil spirits. An orange tree cannot bear a grapefruit, and a spirit of jealousy cannot bear the fruit of a deaf and dumb spirit.

Jesus did not say you would know the spirits by sharing your observations with elders in your church and asking them if they witnessed the same thing. No. Let me tell you, wolves in sheep's clothing make a career of meeting the right people and belonging to the right church. This is the method of the world, and the world will receive them.

How to Try the Spirits

Except for the gifts, there is only one reliable way to try a spirit, which is revealed in Matthew chapter 7. So, how do we try a spirit?

Do men gather grapes of thorns, or figs of thistles? Even so every good tree bringeth forth good fruit; but a corrupt tree bringeth forth evil fruit. A good tree cannot bring forth evil fruit, neither can a corrupt tree bring forth good fruit. Every tree that bringeth not forth good fruit is hewn down, and cast into the fire. **Wherefore by their fruits ye shall know them.**   (Matthew 7:16–20)

Jesus told us that we would know the spirits by their fruits. I believe that the confusion of the body of Christ is this: Instead of using this test to try evil spirits, we have used it to judge the brethren. Jesus was telling us how to try evil spirits whose abodes are in the bodies of men.

We must study the Bible and find out the name of each spirit and what fruit that spirit produces. If we are to correctly try the spirits, we must do it in the biblical way. It takes work, and it takes time.

Most of us are familiar with the fruits of the Holy Spirit. Most Christians agree that it is important to learn them. But what about the fruits of the evil spirits? The Bible says that Satan comes but to steal, kill, and destroy. (See John 10:10.) As we see in Luke 9:55, not knowing the "manner" in which a spirit manifests is offensive to our Lord Jesus. Can you imagine how He must feel when we mistake an evil spirit for His Spirit?

Because we have not been taught the fruits of the evil spirits, many of us do not know the correct way to try a spirit. But now we know the method that cannot fail. If we do it Jesus' way, we will not fail, nor will we be deceived. It is possible, for *"by their fruits [we] shall know them"* (Matthew 7:20).

What if there are no manifestations or fruits? We must either ask for the gift of discerning of Spirits or watch the evil spirits till they bear fruit. In the latter case, a person might think that until he observes the spirit's fruit, he must fellowship with the spirit and give it the benefit of the doubt. But this is not the case. If we commune with the spirit, we may end up in a dangerous situation by the time it begins bearing fruit. We may find that the evil one has constructed many strongholds and fortresses that must be pulled down. Furthermore, communing with an evil spirit may blight the reputation of a Christian.

If, after trial by fruit, you find you are dealing with an evil spirit, treat him like a demon—resist him, bind him, cast him out, and overcome him. Do it aloud if you want, but it is not necessary. You do not need to wrestle a spirit with your mouth; you need to use your mouth only to teach human spirits how to resist evil spirits.

In the book *How to Try a Spirit*, I have listed most of the strongmen and their fruits, as I found them in Scripture, to make it easy for readers to identify and try the spirits. Use this as a resource to indentify and try the spirits to see if they are of God.

Put to the Test

You may be surprised at how many Christian leaders and saints do not know how to try a spirit. I am amazed by the lack of knowledge in the body of Christ. I am going to give an example of such an incident. This is not to criticize or condemn the church but to encourage them to try everything by what is given to us in the Word of God.

I recently attended a meeting to hear an evangelist who is widely advertised and very well known. Before he began his message, he said, "I am going to bind every demon that is in this building and command them to go down the street while we are having this meeting. Therefore, the only spirit that operates in this auditorium is the Holy Spirit." Then he proceeded to pray. Afterward, he told us that anything we would see happening from that moment on would be of the Spirit of God.

Well, I thought, *I'll try them and see.*

After a short message, he called all people who had infirmities to come forward for healing.

Why would he do that? Shouldn't all those spirits be down the street? Surely, those ugly things were not "of the Spirit of God"! The Bible says that spirits of infirmity are evil spirits. So, we can ask ourselves what fruit the evangelist manifested when he said, "The only spirit that operates in this auditorium is the Holy Spirit"? A lying spirit.

Two rows in front of me was a girl of about ten years of age. She was standing up and swaying back and forth like a caged animal, biting her fingers. Every time the evangelist called people to come forward for prayer, she ran to the front. She needed deliverance. Her mother stuffed a handful of tissues in her mouth to keep her from biting her fingers.

How Satan must have laughed! He was having a field day! He was handed the victory, without the slightest struggle. As far as the minister and attendees were concerned, Satan and all of his demons were down the street. Indeed, Satan had pulled off one of his best tricks, all because of ignorance. How pitiful. All the knowledge they needed to try the spirits was in the little black Bible the minister waved above his head. Although there were many pastors, as well as many righteous men and women, in attendance, no one resisted Satan! Why? Because the minister listened to a lying spirit and believed him. The minister lied to the people, and they received it.

> *Beloved, believe not every spirit, but try the spirits whether they are of God.*   (1 John 4:1)

When the minister told the people that the only spirit in the room was the Holy Spirit, Satan had succeeded in deceiving him.

In the little girl, I saw torment, agitation, apprehension, nervous excitement, tension, and stress. She was hyperactive. All of these manifestations are the fruits of a demon of fear. But that was not the only demon she had. There were other fruits being manifested.

She bit herself, gnashed her teeth, and tore at her body, bruising herself. The dumb and deaf spirit was compelling her to hurt herself against her will. All of these manifestations are fruits of the dumb and deaf demon. I know these spirits by their fruit. Those two demons never left the little girl as they were ordered to do.

Then the minister beckoned a young lady in the balcony to come forward. In a hypnotic trance, she rose and slowly made her way to him. He backed up on the stage and exhibited his power over her to make her back up, stand still, or do whatever he commanded her in a hypnotic voice. Then, with screeching cries, the woman fell to the floor. She was possessed with a demon.

She was "slain in the spirit," as they say. Slain in the spirit? What spirit? Did they know the difference between God's Spirit and a spirit of divination? The saints of the Most High God applauded, and the minister bowed. I heard people shout, "Praise the Lord!" "Amen!"

As the people worshiped, I saw more manifestations of the evil spirits. I saw a man with a familiar spirit prophesying. How did I know? By its fruit.[1]

In Deuteronomy 18:9–12, we read,

> *Thou shalt not learn to do after the abominations of those nations. There shall not be found among you any one…that useth divination, or an observer of times, or an enchanter, or a witch, or a charmer, or a consulter with familiar spirits, or a wizard, or a necromancer. For all that do these things are an abomination unto the* Lord.

---

1. See page 38 in *How to Try a Spirit* for a complete listing of the manifestations of the spirit of divination and the familiar spirit.

Anyone who uses these mediums are abominations to the Lord. So why were the saints shouting "Hallelujah!" "Praise you the Lord!"? They should have been resisting the evil spirits and engaging in spiritual warfare. There is a time to praise and a time to fight. We must know when to do each. One thing is for sure: We do not applaud when evil spirits manifest; we fight.

You must learn to decipher between the Spirit of God, the spirits of humans, and evil spirits. Here are some pointers on what to do once you try the spirits:

1. If it is the Holy Spirit, worship and obey Him.

2. If it is the spirit of unredeemed man, loose him from the captivity of Satan and reconcile him to God.

3. If it is the spirit of redeemed man, encourage him, edify him, strengthen, and love him, even as Jesus loves you.

4. If it is an angel, receive him, listen to him, and cooperate with him.

5. If it is Satan, resist him, and he will flee from you. (See James 4:7.)

Beloved, believe not every spirit, but try the spirits whether they are of God. (1 John 4:1)

FOUR

WOLVES IN
SHEEP'S CLOTHING

*"Beware of false prophets, which come to you in sheep's
clothing, but inwardly they are ravening wolves."*
—Matthew 7:15

Have you ever seen signs for fortune-tellers, advisors, healers, and so on? These mediums are not of God and use psychic power. Perhaps you are not likely to go visit a medium or call upon the familiar and divining spirits. But you might allow people in sheepskin come to you because they claim to be Christians. Will you believe them? Will you receive what they have to offer? Or, will you recognize and know these wolves by their fruit?

It is important to know the three kinds of power:

1. God power

2. Satanic power

3.   Psychic power

Ministers who use psychic and satanic power are usually those who are unwilling to submit to the Holy Spirit to be the clean, yielded vessels God desires. I believe that some of them start out with God but then allow sin to come into their lives along the way. Then they find themselves wrapped up in the ways of man. Hundreds of people may gather to hear them, but they stand powerless in their pulpits. God will not anoint them because of sin in their lives. But with all eyes on them, they put on an act. The show must go on! They have a reputation to maintain. They have money to raise. They must fabricate something. At this point, many ministers are willing to resort to divination in order to or make a show of godliness using familiar spirits.

I can see with my "spiritual eyes" exactly how Satan accomplishes these victories in the body of Christ. He wishes to overthrow and seduce our top ministers, but he does not do it overnight.

Yes, Satan knows their vulnerabilities and where to attack them. If he watches them long enough, he will discover their weaknesses. We all have them. Then he analyzes their situations, comes up with a strategy for attack, which involves deciding on which evil spirits to employ, and begins to implement his plan. If these ministers do not know how to try spirits in order to see whether or not they are of God, they will be easy prey.

On the other hand, if ministers recognize their weaknesses and try the spirits by their fruit, they will recognize Satan's attempts to not only knock them out of God's work but also to use them for his purposes. They will not be caught unaware or unprepared but will test and resist the attacks. Satan and his demons will flee from them, but they will not give up altogether—not until they are chained or sent to the pit, where they cease to work.

Satan will not pull these deceived ministers out of the ministry and put them into a witch coven. Oh, no. He deliberately allows them to build their reputations, so that they are well received by the body of Christ. This is one of the reasons why we must know the backgrounds of the ministers we listen to.

While all this is happening, many righteous men and women in the congregation will continue to pray to God in true faith. And we know that *"the effectual fervent prayer of a righteous man availeth much"* (James 5:16). God is bound by His Word to honor them. Therefore, miracles actually take place in the assemblies of deceived ministers. Knowingly or unknowingly, they depend upon the righteous to pray the "prayer of faith" to save the sick.

Witches, warlocks, and false prophets need chants, charms, sacrifices, evil rites, and all kinds of evil, perverted works of the flesh to work for Satan. But, praise God, we worship God in spirit and in truth! (See John 4:24.) Because of the blood sacrifice Jesus made, believers do not need rituals to conjure up authority over the power of evil! Praise and honor and glory be to God for the unspeakable gift of His Son, Jesus Christ!

If you find yourselves under the leadership of a deceived minister, here is what you should do: After you have tried the spirits and found that they are not of God, do not actively participate in the services. Do not join them in worship or prayer. It is possible to become a partaker of the ways of antichrist spirits. If you do not know how to battle these spirits, then walk out!

Jesus said, *"Behold, I send you forth as sheep in the midst of wolves* [false prophets]: *be ye therefore wise as serpents* [knowing not to unduly expose yourself to attacks], *and harmless as doves* [never provoking enmity]" (Matthew 10:16). What a wise analogy Jesus used to teach us this truth! Clear distinction must be drawn between human spirits and evil spirits. If it is a human spirit, you should send forth the spirit of supplication and grace to plead with him, that he may recognize his position and sin, remember the price Jesus paid for him at Calvary, and be led to repentance.

But if it is an evil spirit, launch a powerful counterattack against it. Aim these weapons of God directly at the enemy. They are mighty for pulling down strongholds and nullifying every clever and crafty tactic. Overpower evil; the Spirit that is in you is greater than he that is in the world. (See 1 John 4:4.) Let the people of God arise and His enemies be scattered!

FIVE

CASTING OUT DEVILS

Did you know that Jesus Himself classified the casting out of devils as the gift of working miracles? He did not say that the only ones who could cast them out were those with a deliverance ministry. When you confront a person with an evil spirit, cast the spirit out by the power of God, and point that person toward Jesus, you have worked a miracle! Not only that but you also are employing the works of God!

Let us take a look at a few examples of Christ using this gift.

*And John answered him, saying, Master, we saw one casting out devils in thy name, and he followeth not us: and we forbade him, because he followeth not us. But Jesus said, Forbid him not: for there is no man which shall do a **miracle** in my name, that can lightly speak evil of me.* (Mark 9:38–39)

> *And the people with one accord gave heed unto those things*
> *which Philip spake, hearing and seeing the **miracles** which he*
> *did. For unclean spirits, crying with loud voice, came out of*
> *many that were possessed with them: and many taken with*
> *palsies, and that were lame, were healed.*   (Acts 8:6–7)

How can pastors look into the faces of their congregants who are bound up by devils and refuse to set them free? Are they afraid someone will misunderstand? It there lack of power in the church? Where can they go for help?

If you cast out a devil, the news will quickly spread abroad. Your church building may fill up with people who want to see miracles—signs Jesus gave to us. Then you will have many people to minister to.

If you look through the New Testament, you will find that Jesus told His followers to go and say that the kingdom of heaven is at hand. (See Matthew 10:7.) Then, when they had everyone's attention, they proved it by casting out devils, healing the sick, and raising the dead. (See verse 8.) We, too, must proclaim the message loud and clear, "The kingdom of God has come unto you!" Every devil in hell will shudder.

If you say you are a minister of God, minister His goods! Many who do not believe in deliverance do believe in the gifts of the Holy Spirit and would be happy to perform a miracle.

Denominations who shun the casting out of devils are banning two important gifts of the Holy Spirit—the working of miracles and discerning of spirits. This rejection often stems from a stiff-necked attitude, which Jesus certainly did not have when He dealt with devils.

Being a Christian means to be Christlike in every way: to follow and imitate Christ's example and commands. If Christ performed miracles and cast out demons, then it should be good enough for us.

Some people do not agree with my theology on deliverance from demons. It isn't that I randomly decided to do deliverance. I am *commanded* to do it! I am simply obeying what I am told to do.

The work that He called us to do is to believe God, that we might meet the needs of others by leading them to Christ. This work includes setting the captives free. (See Luke 4:18.)

This was the kind of ministry Jesus had, and it was a well-balanced one. I consider a ministry that refuses to acknowledge and deal with Satan to be an unbalanced one. Jesus dealt with Satan and taught His disciples to do the same. It is important to deal with evil spirits because they are the sources of sin and sickness in this world.

I do not understand how someone can minister to sick people without delivering them from evil spirits, for spirits of infirmity cause all sickness and must be bound before they destroy their hosts. Much of Jesus' ministry was directed against evil spirits. He not only bound the strongmen but He also destroyed their goods. Likewise, ministers of God need to be aggressive against the work of the enemy, using mighty weapons of God to defeat him. Jesus conquered Satan through His death, delivering people out of captivity. Should our work be any less effective? Jesus said it should be greater. *"Verily, verily, I say unto you, He that believeth on me, the works that I do shall he do also; and greater works than these shall he do; because I go unto my Father"* (John 14:12). As one brother put it, "Deliverance is not an addition to the preaching of the gospel, it is the very center of the gospel itself."

Jesus came into the world to set the captives free and to destroy the works of the devil and his demons. (See 1 John 3:8; Isaiah 61:1; Acts 10:38.) I thank God for deliverance.

I hate it when those of us who are faithful to cast out demons are called "demon chasers." It is better to chase them than to run from them like the sons of Sceva did! (See Acts 19:13–16.) Resist the devil, and he will flee from you. (See James 4:7.) But instead of making Satan flee, some Christians are the ones who flee! Remember, we are more than conquerors—not the conquered! (See Romans 8:37.) That is Satan's destiny.

The very reason people don't understand this truth is because they have not seen the miracle of deliverance. There have not been enough instances of deliverance done in public. Casting out demons is one of the signs that should follow believers. (See Mark 16:17.) It what causes unbelievers to believe! Miracles of deliverance are to mark the seal of God's divine authority. Don't tell me they should only be done in private!

There is not one case in the Bible where God's followers went into hiding to cast out a demon. Let the discreet hide in the closet, but let us cast out demons as Jesus did.

And I will give unto thee the keys of the kingdom of heaven: and whatsoever thou shalt bind on earth shall be bound in heaven: and whatsoever thou shalt loose on earth shall be loosed in heaven. Verily I say unto you, Whatsoever ye shall bind on earth shall be bound in heaven: and whatsoever ye shall loose on earth shall be loosed in heaven.
(Matthew 16:19; Matthew 18:18)

SIX

BY WHAT AUTHORITY?

Having spiritual authority means you know who you are in Christ Jesus. It means that you know your correct relationship with the Father and the Son, Jesus Christ, and you know what is yours. All that was wrought upon Calvary and delivered unto the saints is yours. Having spiritual authority means you know what is expected of you, the role you play in the eternal kingdom, and your responsibility toward God.

I was not able to cast out a demon until I knew beyond a doubt that I was supposed to do it; until I searched the Scriptures and found that demons were subject to God's authority in me. I was not able to receive healing for myself or others until God's truth was established in my mind, until I knew that the children's bread is healing. (See Matthew 15:26.) It was this knowledge written in Holy Scriptures that enabled me to pray the prayer of faith to heal the sick. When I found that God commanded me to preach, fast, free the oppressed, undo heavy burdens, cast out demons, heal the sick, and so on, then I was able to obey Him. I knew He had empowered me, through the Holy Spirit, for His work.

The Picture of Authority

When we have spiritual authority, we can see the whole picture *now*, and we can walk in the light of *knowing*. It is in rising above our circumstances that we can exercise spiritual authority. Without spiritual authority, we will have no sense of direction.

Let's look at the picture of authority we are given in the book of Daniel.

A Picture of God

> *I beheld till the thrones were cast down, and the Ancient of days did sit, whose garment was white as snow, and the hair of his head like the pure wool: his throne was like the fiery flame, and his wheels as burning fire. A fiery stream issued and came forth from before him: thousand thousands ministered unto him, and ten thousand times ten thousand stood before him: the judgment was set, and the books were opened. I beheld then because of the voice of the great words which the horn spake: I beheld even till the beast was slain, and his body destroyed, and given to the burning flame.*
>
> (Daniel 7:9–11)

A Picture of Christ

> *I saw in the night visions, and, behold, one like the Son of man came with the clouds of heaven, and came to the Ancient of days, and they brought him near before him. And*

there was given him dominion, and glory, and a kingdom, that all people, nations, and languages, should serve him: his dominion is an everlasting dominion, which shall not pass away, and his kingdom that which shall not be destroyed.

(Daniel 7:13–14)

A Picture of You

But the saints of the most High shall take the kingdom, and possess the kingdom for ever, even for ever and ever....I beheld, and the same horn made war with the saints, and prevailed against them; until the Ancient of days came, and judgment was given to the saints of the most High; and the time came that the saints possessed the kingdom....And the kingdom and dominion, and the greatness of the kingdom under the whole heaven, shall be given to the people of the saints of the most High, whose kingdom is an everlasting kingdom, and all dominions shall serve and obey him.

(Daniel 7:18, 21–22, 27)

Our Ultimate Calling

And from Jesus Christ, who is the faithful witness, and the first begotten of the dead, and the prince of the kings of the earth. Unto him that loved us, and washed us from our sins in his own blood, and hath made us kings and priests unto God and his Father; to him be glory and dominion for ever and ever. Amen.   (Revelation 1:5–6)

And if children, then heirs; heirs of God, and joint-heirs with Christ; if so be that we suffer with him, that we may be also glorified together.   (Romans 8:17)

Now that we know our position, I have a question for you. Will we become rulers over the governments of the world without training? No, we will not!

At a young age, Prince Charles of England entered into a planned, disciplined program of studies and work that were designed to prepare him for his role as the future king of England.

Similarly, God puts His chosen ones through a rigid training to prepare them to carry out His will in the earth. What a marvel it is that every person born into the family of God is born into royalty! Yes, divine royalty! Scripture declares, "[He] *hath translated us into the kingdom of his dear Son*" (Colossians 1:13). Being born into the royal family gives us the right to use the divine name—Jesus Christ!

"*Make straight in the desert a highway for our God*" (Isaiah 40:3.) By bearing God's message and comforting others with what He's given us, we are making straight in the dry desert a highway for God. We may not realize it, but we are preparing a path for the Lord as His messengers. I believe that our service to God in coming ages is largely determined by the manner in which we exercise our ministries before Him now.

"Those who do not know Christ should realize that death does not end all…'*It is appointed unto men once to die, and after this the judgment*' (Hebrews 9:27). Christians, too, need to be aware that death does not end our service to Him [The devil uses this idea to make you passive]. We are to continue as servants of Jehovah throughout the eternal ages, reigning with Him and serving Him forever and ever, and we are being prepared for that service right here and now."

But when we face trials, we often ask, What is the purpose of it all? For quite some time now, I have asked myself this question. And my quest to understand the purpose of God in my life has been met with wisdom from above. I have found the answer! Just like Prince Charles had to train for a future position as king, so we, too, have to train as God's followers.

I am sure that we would not be willing to go through such rigid training without any sort of compensation. But if we knew that the things we had to give up in our personal lives were to prepare us for our ultimate reign as kings and queens, we might be more willing to do so. Wouldn't the trials that purify us be easier to bear if we understood their purpose?

> *The Spirit itself beareth witness with our spirit, that we are the children of God: and if children, then heirs; heirs of God, and joint-heirs with Christ; if so be that we suffer with him, that we may be also glorified together. For I reckon that the sufferings of this present time are not worthy to be compared with the glory which shall be revealed in us.*
>
> (Romans 8:16–18)

The saints are going to share in the glory, all right! We know from studying the Scriptures on the kingdom of God that we are given authority to rule on earth with the goods He gave to us when He ascended to heaven. Christ's goods have been given to us already, and if we rule well over what He has given us, He will give us much more. (See Luke 16:10.)

To "rule" is to govern, control, direct, manage, command, and decree. We can rule, or have complete dominion, in His stead, doing His work with His authority!

Realize how necessary it is for you to rule over evil spirits, commanding them in the name of Jesus with a rod of iron. (See Revelation 2:27.)

God has big plans for us! We are in the Holy Spirit's school of intensive training. He puts us through a program designed to condition us for our high calling. The program for Prince Charles was ordered by Queen Elizabeth and the many royal rulers that preceded her reign. Our training has been ordered by the King of all kings, and it is His good pleasure to give us the kingdom. This world belongs to our Father, and all the fullness thereof.

> *But the saints of the most High shall take the kingdom, and possess the kingdom for ever, even for ever and ever....I beheld, and the same horn made war with the saints, and prevailed against them; until the Ancient of days came, and judgment was given to the saints of the most High; and the time came that the saints possessed the kingdom....And the kingdom and dominion, and the greatness of the kingdom under the whole heaven, shall be given to the people of the saints of the most High, whose kingdom is an everlasting kingdom, and all dominions [and rulers] shall serve and obey him.*   (Daniel 7:18, 21–22, 27)

We will be ruling *all* dominions! And the things Jesus gave us to rule over is only a fraction of what He will give us in the everlasting kingdom.

So, friends, let us enter into this ministry with submission to God, so that He may prepare us, making us fit vessels, for this high calling in Christ Jesus!

SEVEN

FIGHT A GOOD FIGHT

It is important for born-again Christians to realize that they are involved in a battle against the enemy and that they will never reach their goals of spiritual progress—the crown of life, and the prize of the high calling that are in Christ Jesus—without tremendous struggle. *"Shall your brethren go to war, and shall ye **sit** here?"* (Numbers 32:6).

If you intend to be one of those who sit on the fence—remaining neutral and never wrestling the powers and principalities of the world to win blood-bought victories—you will probably never hear the words from Jesus "Well done, my good and faithful servant!" (See Matthew 25:21, 23.) If you are busy opposing those who are wrestling and casting out devils, you may hear the words "Depart from me, you worker of iniquity!" (See Matthew 7:23; Luke 13:27.)

Many would like to accept only the love and rewards of God and leave the fighting to others. But this cannot be! You may get by without fighting if you wish, but the evil spirits are not going to stop fighting back. If you want to give up, go ahead and surrender unconditionally. They will gladly take you captive. They will enslave you and use you for Satan's will. But this is not the will of the Lord. He said to resist the devil, giving him no place in your life. He said that He gave you power over the devil and his demons. (See Luke 10:19.) But it is up to *you* to use it.

We are already in a period of terrible warfare—terrible because we are fighting unseen forces; terrible because, in spite of the training resources God has given us, we are shirking our responsibility to prepare themselves and others for war; terrible because we, for the most part, are unprepared to war in the spiritual realm. What will be the results? Many will not finish their course. They will be defeated and deceived by evil spirits. (See 1 Timothy 4:1–2.)

What I am saying to you is this: Whether or not you fight may seem like your choice, but it is not. War has already been declared and is now raging. Every conflict that comes your way is a chance for you to win a victory over the devil.

The Battle of the Ages Is On

Truly, the battle is fought in the soul of man. We are fighting for control of our thoughts, emotions, wills, and faith.

No country ever goes to war without first declaring war upon another country and stating its reasons for doing so. Yet some of us blindly relinquish our faith without so much as a struggle! It is not pleasing to Christ Jesus for us to give up at the onset of battle, or at all! Those who overcome to the end will be rewarded. (See Revelation 2:10.)

Paul demonstrates the power of God along the course of his journey. Those who withstood the gospel by asserting themselves against Paul and Peter were led away blind or carried away dead! This may seem a bit harsh to you, but this is the way of war. It is not a Sunday picnic. Wars are won by…

1. force

2. strength

3. resistance

4. power

The Enemy has come to kill, steal, and destroy. (See John 10:10.) If we do not fight and win, Satan and his evil spirits will accomplish their mission!

Paul was a soldier of the cross of Jesus Christ. So are we, or so we should be. Paul knew how to fight a good fight. First, he fought in the flesh, persecuting, threatening, and imprisoning many of Christ's followers. He warred such a good fight that God said to him, *"Saul, Saul, why persecutest thou me?"* (Acts 9:4). Now that is some kind of fighter! After Paul encountered God on the road to Damascus, he then excelled in spiritual warfare. He defected to the other side and fought for a different Master.

Before his conversion, Paul had authority from the chief priest to bind all who called on the name of Jesus. But after his conversion, he had authority from the Chief Priest Jesus to bind all who opposed His name. He said that he had fought a good fight, and indeed he did! (See 2 Timothy 4:7.)

What kind of fight are we putting up? Puny! In some cases, pitiful! Most certainly, much of our efforts are not fit for the Master! A good warrior is a person who can engage in splendid warfare and win victories over the enemy—victories fit for our Lord Jesus Christ that will solicit a "well done" from the Lord.

Our aim as soldiers is to satisfy the One who enlisted us, that is, Christ.

The book of Revelation reveals that Paul fought to win. In 1 Corinthians 9:26, he said that he did not fight *"as one that beateth the air,"* but as one with purpose, to win!

How often I see my brethren "beat the air." They don't bother to find out who they are fighting or what they are fighting for. Imagine if the president of the United States after the attack at Pearl Harbor did not know whom to launch a counterattack against. What if the United States had declared war on France instead of Japan, beating the air? Wouldn't our victory be more certain if we learned about our enemy—his position, strengths, and weaknesses—so we knew how to defeat him?

Identify the Enemy

One of the first things we have to do then in spiritual warfare is to identify the enemy.

Evil Spirits

> For we wrestle not against flesh and blood [people], but against principalities, against powers, against the rulers of the darkness of this world, against spiritual wickedness in high places.   (Ephesians 6:12)

Notice that we are the ones who are expected to wrestle. We are not fighting against people but unseen forces—evil spirits. We are fighting against principalities—rulers, leaders, executives, chiefs, heads, masterminds, strongmen, and their powers, tricks, strategies, and craftiness. (See Ephesians 6:11–12.)

We are told in 2 Corinthians 2:11 that we are not to be ignorant of these devices, lest Satan take advantage of us. It is to our advantage to know who our enemy is, how he works, and how he attacks.

The strongmen are the cause of all darkness in this world. We should not be as concerned with defeating their works as we are with defeating them. Even if you were successful in stopping their plans, you have not addressed the main source of the problem. (See Matthew 12:29–30.)

If not opposed, strongmen will wear down the saints. They will have no mercy on us; they will use all their power and strength against us. They do not fight as men who beat the air; they fight with purpose to win!

Human Spirits

In addition to the strongmen listed in *How to Try a Spirit*, there are also human spirits who have rejected Christ and chosen to follow Satan. They are in need of deliverance. But they must be bound and dealt with by believers, because they are high-ranking principal forces in the satanic kingdom. They control and direct demons, and exist in our world as witches, mediums, fortune-tellers, psychics, magicians, and sorcerers.

Let us look at the apostle Paul's encounter with Elymas the sorcerer, that we might learn how to deal with such an enemy.

And when they had gone through the isle unto Paphos, they found a certain sorcerer, a false prophet, a Jew, whose name was Barjesus: which was with the deputy of the country, Sergius Paulus, a prudent man; who called for Barnabas and Saul, and desired to hear the word of God. But Elymas the sorcerer (for so is his name by interpretation) withstood them, seeking to turn away the deputy from the faith. Then Saul, (who also is called Paul,) filled with the Holy Ghost, set his eyes on him, and said, O full of all subtlety and all

*mischief, thou child of the devil, thou enemy of all right-
eousness, wilt thou not cease to pervert the right ways of the
Lord? And now, behold, the hand of the Lord is upon thee,
and thou shalt be blind, not seeing the sun for a season. And
immediately there fell on him a mist and a darkness; and he
went about seeking some to lead him by the hand. Then the
deputy, when he saw what was done, believed, being astonished at the doctrine of the Lord.* (Acts 13:6–12)

These verses lay out a spiritual war over faith. How did Paul
fight the battle? He did not pat Elymas on the back and try to
win him for the Lord. He didn't sing praises. He didn't turn his
cheek. He tried the spirit, found it to be evil, and treated it like a
devil. He quickly identified him as the enemy and then exercised
the power and authority delegated to him. We cannot judge the
brethren, but we can judge devils!

What happened to Elymas? Darkness fell on him and he
began looking for someone to lead him. God backed up Paul's
words with power from on high! We need to demonstrate the
same power of God to usher in the kingdom. When the deputy
saw what had happened, they were astonished and believed!
Merriam Webster's 11th Collegiate Dictionary defines *astonish* as
"to strike with sudden and usually great wonder or surprise." We
need to astound more people.

It is going to take more than the measly sermonette "Jesus
loves you, anyhow!" to walk victoriously. Jesus hates discourage-
ment, and He wants us to walk in His deliverance from it! We
need to do as the church at Antioch was doing when the Holy
Spirit said, "*Separate me Barnabas and Saul for the work where-
unto I have called them*" (Acts 13:2). Does this mean the Holy
Spirit called them to blind Elymas? Yes. But Christians are only
supposed to do good, you say. That *was* good. Yes, we need to

come together and fast and pray until we hear from heaven. We need more than the spiritual high that comes from stamping our feet, clapping our hands, and saying to others, "Jesus loves you." We need to speak with such power of the Spirit of God that our enemies rise up and strike us, as they did to Stephen!

The deputy was astonished at the doctrine of the Lord. The blinding of Elymas was a good and righteous work—the right way to fight the devil and win!

Paul Said to Fight

Fight the good fight of faith, lay hold on eternal life, where-unto thou art also called, and hast professed a good profession before many witnesses.   (1 Timothy 6:12)

Paul did not mince his words when warning the enemy. He addressed him not as a mere man walking in the flesh. Although Paul walked in the flesh, he did not fight like a human being. The weapons he used were not of men, such as clubs, spears, swords, darts, arrows, and so on, but mighty weapons of God! He expressed hope that he wouldn't have to show them how harsh and rough he could be, for he was not as weak as he may have appeared. The plans and methods he used to win his battles were not of human origin. They were supernatural weapons belonging to almighty God Himself!

Wow! I most certainly would not want to come up against a man like Paul, would you? Every demon in Corinth must have fled in terror before he arrived! Could it be that we are too mealy-mouthed when using our authority in Jesus' name?

Paul said that God's mighty weapons could:

1. "*Break down every proud argument against God*" (2 Corinthians 10:5 TLB).

2. *"Break down every wall that can be built to keep men from finding* [God]*"* (2 Corinthians 10:5 TLB).

3. *"Capture rebels and bring them back to God"* (verse 5 TLB).

4. *"Change* [the rebels] *into men whose hearts' desire is obedience to Christ"* (verse 5 TLB).

Paul said that he intended to use these weapons against every rebel who remained after he first used them against the Corinthians. (See 2 Corinthians 10:6 TLB). Is that a fair way to fight? Well, nevertheless, he said to them, *"The trouble with you is that you look at me and I seem weak and powerless, but you don't look beneath the surface. Yet if anyone can claim the power and authority of Christ, I certainly can"* (2 Corinthians 10:7, TLB). Anyone can use the mighty weapons God has provided for His church.

Wouldn't they help us in our warfare? Then let us find out what they are and how to use them.

The Powerful, Mighty Weapons of God

Without God and His mighty weapons, we are fighting unconquerable forces! But, He has given us:

1. His Dominion

He gave us dominion over all evil forces. *"The spirits are subject unto you"* (Luke 10:20). They must mind every word you say. If spirits are not minding you, you are probably not ordering them! We are supposed to tell them what to do and where to go. The devil and all his forces don't stand a chance against a believer with God-given dominion!

2. His Spirit

When Jesus ascended to heaven, He gave gifts to men. He prayed to the Father, and the He gave us the same Spirit Jesus used when He delivered His people!

3.   His Name

Jesus said, *"In my name shall they cast out devils; they shall speak with new tongues; they shall take up serpents; and if they drink any deadly thing, it shall not hurt them; they shall lay hands on the sick, and they shall recover"* (Mark 16:17–18).

4.   His Blood

Jesus shed His blood for the remission of sins, so that we are justified in the sight of God. Because of the blood, we can enter God's presence.[2] (See Hebrews 10:19.) With it, we are too powerful for the devil. We are marvelously equipped for the struggle, because we are more than conquerors! (See Romans 8:37.)

5.   His Strength

You can do all things through Christ who strengthens you. Without Him, we can do nothing, but with Him, there is nothing we cannot do. (See Philippians 4:13.)

6.   His Word

When we speak the Word, we send it forth to accomplish what it says! *"Unto us a child is born"* (Isaiah 9:6). *"Unto us"*? Yes, we have Jesus—all that He is and was!

7.   His Flesh

And as they were eating, Jesus took bread, and blessed it, and brake it, and gave it to the disciples, and said, Take, eat; this is my body. And he took the cup, and gave thanks, and gave it to them, saying, Drink ye all of it; for this is my blood of the new testament, which is shed for many for the remission of sins.

(Matthew 26:26–28; see Mark 14:22–24)

---

2. See chapter 15, "The Way into the Kingdom of God."

8. His Life

   [Jesus] *died for us, that, whether we wake or sleep, we should live together with him.* (1 Thessalonians 5:10)

9. His Mind

   For who hath known the mind of the Lord, that he may instruct him? But we have the mind of Christ.
   (1 Corinthians 2:16)

10. His Wisdom

    If any of you lack wisdom, let him ask of God, that giveth to all men liberally, and upbraideth not; and it shall be given him. (James 1:5)

11. His Knowledge

    According as his divine power hath given unto us all things that pertain unto life and godliness, through the knowledge of him that hath called us to glory and virtue. (2 Peter 1:3)

12. His Power

    For God hath not given us the spirit of fear; but of power, and of love, and of a sound mind. (1 Timothy 1:7)

13. His Joy

    These things have I [Jesus] spoken unto you, that my joy might remain in you, and that your joy might be full.
    (John 15:11)

    And now come I to thee; and these things I speak in the world, that they might have my joy fulfilled in themselves.
    (John 17:13)

14. His Counsel

But the Comforter (Counselor, Helper, Intercessor, Advocate, Strengthener, Standby), the Holy Spirit, Whom the Father will send in My name [in My place, to represent Me and act on My behalf], He will teach you all things.

(John 14:26 AMP)

15. His Armor

Put on the whole armour of God, that ye may be able to stand against the wiles of the devil.   (Ephesians 6:11)

16. His Work

Verily, verily, I say unto you, He that believeth on me, the works that I do shall he do also; and greater works than these shall he do; because I go unto my Father.   (John 14:12)

17. His Image

So God created man in his own image, in the image of God created he him; male and female created he them.

(Genesis 1:27)

18. His Reward

The LORD render to every man his righteousness and his faithfulness.   (1 Samuel 26:23)

19. His Inheritance

Ye were sealed with that holy Spirit of promise, which is the earnest of our inheritance until the redemption of the purchased possession, unto the praise of his glory.

(Ephesians 1:13–14)

EIGHT

KEEP THE FAITH

What are we fighting for? Jude said, *"Ye should earnestly contend for the faith"* (Jude 1:3). The powers of darkness are fighting to overthrow, dilute, and divert our faith, and to convince us, if possible, of the contrary. Paul said to *"fight"*:

> *Fight the good fight of faith, lay hold on eternal life, whereunto thou art also called, and hast professed a good profession before many witnesses.*   (1 Timothy 6:12)

Know what God said and believe it. Obey Him, regardless of how impossible or foolish it may seem. Agree with Him that His estimations are true estimations. God wants us to know that He is faithful to His Word, watching over it to see that it accomplishes everything it is was sent to do. (See Jeremiah 1:12.) He meant exactly what He said, so reject and cast off all that is contrary to His Word.

Why Fight for Faith?

Through faith, we:

1. Subdue kingdoms of darkness (See Hebrews 11:33.)

2. Wrought righteousness (See verse 13.)

3. Obtain promises, like the benefits and power of the kingdom of God (See verse 13.)

4. Stop the mouths of lions by taking dominion over evil spirits and locking the jaws of liars. (See verse 13.)

5. Quench the violence of fire, as when the Hebrew children were neither scorched nor burned (See verse 34.)

6. Escape the edge of the sword (See verse 14.)

7. Are made strong (See verse 14.)

8. Are empowered in battle (See verse 14.)

9. Make enemies flee (See verse 14.)

If the enemy can test and try our faith, then he can stop us from doing all of these things!

The Meaning of Faith

What is faith? When a person has faith, he strictly adheres to the Word of God. He is "glued" to God's laws, so that contrary evidence to His promises, doctrines, and covenants do not move him. He places total trust in the covenant maker God!

He believes God's principles are supreme. They are the highest authority in his life. He relies on the everlasting truth, as opposed to any other principle, authority, or doctrine. He is completely loyal to the Lord and carefully observes his thoughts and acts to ensure they are subject to God.

He is a bond servant of our sovereign Lord and King. He is not fickle, unsteady, or easily deceived.

Keep the Faith

The first and foremost goal of evil spirits is to break down our faith. For example, when the spirit of infirmity attacks a person, it attacks his body along with his faith in divine healing. Satan tries to get us to doubt that we are healed by Christ's stripes. So, each time you encounter spiritual conflict, try the spirits by their fruit. Know who you are fighting and ask yourself what is at stake. Along with other things, your faith will be on the line.

Let's be ready, so that we can say with Paul,

*I have fought a good fight, I have finished my course, I have kept the **faith**: Henceforth there is laid up for me a crown of righteousness, which the Lord, the righteous judge, shall give me at that day: and not to me only, but unto all them also that love his appearing.* (2 Timothy 4:7–8)

"FAITH IN GOD"

You have been given power to preach the gospel,
Heal the sick, cast out devils, raise the dead,
Disappear in a riot, walk on water,
and feed the multitude without bread.
If you have faith of a mustard seed,
You can pull up a tree as if it were a weed,
Or remove a mountain and plant it in the sea.
You need only to believe in Me.
How long will I be with you to teach and to train?
Listen closely now, while I tell you again:
Remember the loaves and the fishes,
and try your best to understand
That My work does not depend upon the laws of nature,
or of man!
How long will you suffer before you will know?
I am the Son of God, I have told you so.

By *Mary Garrison*

NINE

SATAN AND
HIS DEMONS MUST FLEE

*"Submit yourselves therefore to God.
Resist the devil, and he will flee from you."*
—James 4:7

When we submit ourselves to God, put on the whole armor, take up our mighty weapons, put on faith, and resist the devil, evil spirits must flee, run, retreat, or surrender. If the latter, we can capture them and punish them.

Be alert. When you are attacked, pay close attention to what is happening—what you see, hear, and think. Also take note of what is being threatened. By knowing our battles and being on guard, we can be victorious in our lives and help others to do the same. We do not have to tolerate evil spirits, allowing them to work unhindered. We can test them by their fruit, then bind them, cast them out, and destroy their goods. Ask the Holy Spirit to help you develop the fruits of righteousness.

Remember that this is not a work of the flesh but of the spirit. The demons do not have to have permission to entice, seduce, and deceive. Jesus dealt with evil spirits, wherever and whenever they crossed His path. He instructed us to take dominion over them as well. They have no rights, but we have *every* right as people who belong to the Father. We do not have to tolerate them. We can dismiss them.

TEN

SEDUCING SPIRIT

"Now the Spirit speaks expressly, that in the latter times some shall depart from the faith, giving heed to seducing spirits, and doctrines of devils; speaking lies in hypocrisy; having their conscience seared with a hot iron."
—1 Timothy 4:1–2

Manifestations of the seducing spirit:

- Seared conscience
- Seduction
- Enticement
- Temptation
- Allurement
- Excitement
- Interest

- Fascination

- Attractiveness

- Arousal

- Deceit

A seducing spirit is an evil emissary of Satan that is sent to overthrow a person and take him into captivity. Having accomplished that task, he then turns his victim over to another evil spirit, such as a deceiving spirit, a lying spirit, a perverse spirit, and so on. We could say that the seducing spirit is a "forerunner" of many others. His purpose is to sear the conscience, seducing through temptation and allurement and winning people over. Then another evil spirit can take up where the seducing spirit left off.

How does he do this? The seducing spirit will carefully select a yielded victim and locate his or her biggest weaknesses, such as lust, greed, pride, and so on. Then he will unceasingly play upon these weaknesses by tempting that person to sin. The seducing spirit can inflict his blow only if the victim doesn't resist his advances!

Seducing spirits know that people have within them the ability to know God the right way. This knowledge of God is seated in what we call "conscience." The Bible says that seducing spirits burn or sear the conscience, as if with a hot iron. (See 1 Timothy 4:2.) *Merriam Webster's 11th Collegiate Dictionary* defines *sear* as "to cause withering or drying" or "to burn, scorch, mark, or injure with or as if with sudden application of intense heat." Seducing spirits make us hard, calloused, and insensible to what is right and wrong. It renders the conscience unable to rebuke, condemn, and effectively resist dark forces.

Now the victim has an open wound that is susceptible to "germs." Furthermore, his immune system is not able to resist infection.

Take Heed

Christians must not be gullible. Demons try to trick, cheat, and defraud us. Jesus took great steps to warn us of this, saying, *"Take ye heed: behold, I have foretold you all things"* (Mark 13:23). And He has! We just don't always seek to know them as we should.

To avoid being seduced, try the spirits to see if they are of God. Dot not be foolish or assume that all spirits are of God. Notice the fruits, pay close attention, and then take authority over everything that sets itself up against God.

How to Loose Those Who Are Seduced

Bind strongmen by calling them by name.

For example, the seducing spirit may be ousted from two bodies, both of the seducer and seduced, in which he lives and operates. We must command him to leave and not to come back.

Then we must address *all* the damage he has done—his goods. There is the deceived victim, with his or her messed-up life, perhaps a head full of error, a broken home, a separated family—evil habits as a result of the fruit of one or more demons.

As you can see, there is far more work involved than just dealing with the destroyers, the strongmen, although dealing with them is the first of our duties. And it is the easiest of all. After we have bound the strongmen, Jesus says that we are then to destroy their goods. (See 2 Corinthians 10:6.)

The Charge of Ephesians 5

Before casting out a demon, we are to bring to light all the works of darkness, so that we can clearly see them and deal with them. Then we must call in ministering spirits to occupy the empty place until a complete healing can be accomplished. We can minister to these people by administering oil, practicing the laying on of the hands, and offering up prayers of faith.

As children of light (see Ephesians 5:8), we have a right to bring to light what we suspect to be hidden acts of evil, studying them closely so that we may prove what is acceptable unto the Lord. (See verse 10.)

When we see them in the light of truth, we are better able to decide if they are of Christ by, in some cases, reproving them.

We might pray along these lines:

I command that all of the works done in secret places of darkness and hidden from eyes, shameful even to be spoken of, as well as the works of all evil spirits involved, human or demonic, be made manifest (exposed, shown clearly) to me, that I may clearly see them.

We expose what is ungodly and bring it into the light through our prayers of rebuke, with which we charge and attack evil works and forces. Then we must be prepared for what follows, knowing the proper action to take.

In Ephesians 5:11, we are told to stop fellowshipping with unfruitful works of darkness that are done in secret or mystery.

Last but not least, after repentance, we must preach the gospel truth to seal the deliverance and completely free the victim. As you can see, we have much to do in the spirit realm. Our first work can be done silently and from any place. Though there is much work to be done, remember that you are not the only ones on a particular case. God has a mighty army that is ready for battle.

Are they not all ministering spirits, sent forth to minister for them who shall be heirs of salvation?   (Hebrews 1:14)

Send them forth!

ELEVEN

WISDOM FOR THE SEDUCED AND DECEIVED

When I wrote *How to Try a Spirit*, I did not teach on seducing or deceiving spirits, because God had not yet revealed to me their fruits and works. But I now know the truth that can lead people into victory. John tells us, *"Ye shall know the truth, and the truth shall set you free"* (John 8:32). Praise God!

A Story of Deliverance

I once ministered to a couple who were involved in an occult group. The man was not as involved in the group as the woman. Through a Christian worker, he came to know God, but his wife remained in a state of apparent hopelessness. He took her to many churches and ministers in hopes that she could be freed from the occult, but it seemed there was no one who could help her. He prayed, fasted, and asked the Holy Spirit to guide him.

One night, as he sat in a large auditorium listening to an evangelist, he noticed two ladies in front of him passing a book back and forth and discussing it. He knew by the quickening of the Holy Spirit that the book would contain the help he so desperately needed. He boldly told the ladies that he must have it. One of them sold him her copy. It was *How to Try a Spirit*. After reading it, he was filled with hope that his wife could be freed, and he set out to find me.

I told the man that a person involved in false religion must be willing to submit to the long-term ministry of healing, deliverance, and teaching, if they wanted to be completely freed. Knowledge of the Word of truth is a safeguard against further deception. (See 1 Timothy 4:1.)

Many are willing to submit to physicians and psychiatrists over long periods of time, but few are willing to a long-term submission to sound doctrine. It is difficult to unlearn what has been learned. But false teaching must be dislodged. It must gradually be replaced with the doctrines of Christ. The person who wants to be freed must submit themselves to sound teaching and learning the Bible.

I told this couple that they would not be freed after a couple of sessions but that they must faithfully submit to God until they receive the truth of the Word and walk in it. They agreed and were very faithful in attending all the meetings.

After much prayer and teaching, the woman was still possessed. She continuously complained of a "numb" feeling in her head. It seemed that no matter how much we ministered to her, something still stood in the way. We desperately needed some special knowledge—a revelation from God.

One day, I was in the city where the headquarters of this particular occult group was located. I was sitting at a stoplight when I saw dozens of young students walking out of a building across the intersection in front of me. They looked as if they had been seduced by lies, and I assumed they had been studying occult practices, probably the same cult this couple had been involved with. As I looked at their clean-cut, young faces, I cried out to the Lord, "God, help us help them!" For some reason, we could not stand up against this demon's power.

Praise God, He heard me from His holy hill! That very instant, it felt as though a curtain had been raised, and I saw the wiles of the devil. I saw the strategies of those lying spirits. I knew their innermost secrets; I knew the truth about them! Glory! And I was confident this truth would release the poor lady, and who knew how many others. Perhaps multitudes of deceived people would be delivered and healed.

I drove back to the motel I was staying at and propped myself up in bed with a pencil and sheet of paper. God had shown me how the enemy had been working all day long, because He knew their every move. God gazes upon their activities and confuses their efforts.

The Bible says that the Holy Spirit will take the secret things of the Father and show them to us. Glory to God in the highest, who sees that His servants lack no good gift! Victory! The Lord said,

> And I will give thee the treasures of darkness, and hidden riches of secret places, that thou mayest know that I, the LORD, which all thee by thy name, am the God of Israel.
> (Isaiah 45:3)

Then I could clearly see why the man's wife had not been completely restored. After we had bound the strongman and loosed the woman, she still had a horribly wounded conscience. She had been "burned" by the infection of lies and false doctrine. She had lost her ability to tell right from wrong. You can see why it seemed impossible for her to be freed without outside help.

I believe that the numb feeling she experienced was because of her seared and wounded conscience. Casting out the demon is the easiest part of deliverance. Dealing with the damage left behind is the difficult part. In this case, the woman needed healing. Her conscience needed restoration, so that she could actively rebuke and resist the dark forces of the cult. Until this vital healing took place, she could not hold on to deliverance, even if she received it.

All Are Searching

Every human being, especially the young, is on a quest. Everyone knows there is much more to life than what meets the eye. The Bible says that things that are seen are temporal and things unseen are eternal. (See 2 Corinthians 4:18.) Think on this. We may seek the Holy Spirit but find an unholy spirit.

The Holy Spirit often leads seekers of truth to various ministries, where they sit in pews and are bored by the programs and services. If they do not receive the spiritual help they seek, they will look elsewhere for it.

Satan is not idle. In fact, he is very involved in our quest for truth. He dispatches seducing spirits to lead seekers astray. These spirits always do the same thing, even though their approaches differ from person to person.

I do not know how long it takes seducing spirits to burn or sear the conscience. But I do know that if a person listens to the lies of the deceiving spirit and does not resist him, he will be deceived. The spirit will brand his conscience with an iron

This is why Jesus has given us the infallible test—trying the spirits by their fruits.

TWELVE

HOW SEDUCING AND PERVERSE SPIRITS MINISTER TO HOMOSEXUALS

There was a man I once knew who was gay. I do not profess to know or understand what dark circumstances happened in his life to cause him to become a homosexual. I do not know the terrible battles he had been dealt to cause such deep wounds that would not heal. Hurt and lonely, he withdrew from society.

I will write about what I do know to be true. I do so in the hopes of ministering healing truth to those who were injured and who, for some reason or another, have become homosexual. I hope that this truth would unlock the doors of freedom for them. As I present this truth, please remember that all good salve stings when it is applied to open wounds. So stand firm, no matter how much it hurts. The loving Father has His arms open wide, offering healing for the bruised and broken.

Homosexuals, like every other sinner, are created in the likeness of God. Yes, the Father of all spirits puts within them a clear understanding of the invisible things that *He* has made. They are born with a built-in knowledge of God's eternal power and godhead. They probably have never realized how valuable they are to the Creator. Perhaps they have cried out to Him many times in the dregs of despair, "Why?" And perhaps they have not heard that before the foundations of the earth were laid, God the Father longed for children. He created all people in His image for the purpose of living in fellowship with them. Because of this, He gave all people intellect and free will to choose Him. He created man for His own pleasure. (See Revelation 4:11.)

But there is another side to this picture—Satan. He knows how valuable men and women are to God, and he desires to turn them away from their Creator. So he has laid certain snares for them. Many homosexuals assume that they became gay on their own, with no outside intervention. They have been deceived. They are in a cell without bars—but there is a key. If they receive the truth, they will be set free. Remember, truth is the *only* key.

Here is how homosexuality occurs: At least two highly trained emissaries are sent by Satan to a specific person. A seducing spirit will do his job first, searing the conscience to render it unable to function, and, if he succeeds, he will call in a stronger spirit, such as a perverse spirit, to take over where he left off and imprison that person. If that person participates in unseemly acts that are unnatural, ignoring their conscience, which tells them that God made male for female, then the seducing spirit has succeeded in wounding this person, and the perverse spirit can begin his evil task.

Now, the perverse spirit also has a plan and wastes no time in putting it into action. His first work is to wound the human spirit. How does he do it? Does he use an abusive father? A terrible rejection by the opposite sex? Only he knows. But, no matter how it is accomplished, he deals that person a heavy blow. The damage is done.

Now this terrible wound corrupts the person, causing him or her to:

1. Rebel against God

2. Hate God

3. Fret

4. Dishonor their body

5. Disobey their parents

6. Pervert gospel truth

7. Surrender to wickedness, causing him or her to later despise him- or herself.

Finally, the perverse spirit will lead the victim into a sinful life. *"They were fully aware of God's death penalty for these crimes, yet they went right ahead and did them anyway and encouraged others to do them, too"* (Romans 1:32 TLB).

Now it is time for the good news, God has provided a way of escape for the victim. Help lies in a true conversion and a decision to commit oneself to Christ. This involves binding the seducing and perverse spirits and casting them out. Call upon the name of Jesus.

*For God so loved the world, that he gave his only begotten Son, that whosoever believeth in Him should **not** perish, but have everlasting life. For God sent not his Son into the world to condemn the world; but that the world through him might be saved.* (John 3:16–17)

*Behold the **Lamb of God**, which taketh away the sin of the world.* (John 1:29)

When we acknowledge our sin and accept Jesus Christ as our Savior, God gives us a new nature. We are born again. "*Verily, verily, I say unto thee, Except a man be born again, he cannot see the kingdom of God*" (John 3:3). When we accept Christ as our Lord, we receive eternal life, for "*as many as received him, to them gave he power to become the sons of God, even to them that believe on his Name*" (John 1:12).

He that believeth on the Son hath everlasting life: and he that believeth not the Son shall not see life; but the wrath of God abideth on him. (John 3:36)

*Verily, verily, I say unto you, He that heareth my word, and believeth on him that sent me, hath everlasting life, and shall not come into condemnation; but **is passed from death unto life**.* (John 5:24)

Now that you have heard this Word, could you say to Jesus, "You have suffered in vain for me, but no thank you"? Choose this day whom you will serve. I implore you, choose life.

Know ye not that the unrighteous shall not inherit the kingdom of God? Be not deceived: neither fornicators, nor idolaters, nor adulterers, nor effeminate, nor abusers of themselves with mankind, nor thieves, nor covetous, nor drunkards, nor revilers, nor extortioners, shall inherit the kingdom of God. And such were some of you: but ye are washed, but ye are sanctified, but ye are justified in the name of the Lord Jesus, and by the Spirit of our God. (1 Corinthians 6:9–11)

Such mercy!

THIRTEEN

FAMILIAR SPIRITS

*"Thou shalt not learn to do after the abominations of those nations. There shall not be found among you **any one** that...useth divination, or an observer of times, or an enchanter, or a witch, or a charmer, or a consulter with **familiar spirits**, or a wizard, or a necromancer. For **all** that do these things are an abomination unto the Lord."*
—Deuteronomy 18:9–12

*T*he New Unger's Bible Dictionary defines familiar spirit as "a divining demon present in the physical body of the conjurer.... The term *familiar* is used to describe the demon because it was regarded by the English translators as a servant ("famulus"), belonging to the family ("familiaris"), who was on intimate terms with and might be readily summoned by the one possessing it."[3]

---

3. Merrill F. Unger, *The New Unger's Bible Dictionary* (Chicago, IL: Moody Press, 1988), 399.

Satan imitates the truth, assigning familiar spirits to overthrow and bring family members into Satan's kingdom.

Before a person who has the familiar spirit dies, he or she can decide which family member will receive the familiar spirit. This may be called receiving a veil or mantle, a counterfeit anointing.

I have ministered to women who have "received the mantle," or this familiar spirit, at the deathbed of their mothers. They were told to receive it and felt it come into them as their mothers died. A few of them were told that they were born with a "veil" over them and would be empowered to divine acts by the familiar spirit.

Familiar spirits will stay within a bloodline until the family dies out, or until they are cast out or resisted. Only then will they seek another family to possess. Sometimes, when familiar spirits are detected, renounced, and cast out of a family, they will enter into some of the family's possessions, such as livestock, in order to stay within the family. Then they will try to enter back in by catching family members off guard.

If not resisted continually, these foreboding spirits will come and go as they please. They may leave but are readily summoned by a medium. They are on intimate terms with the person possessed, anxious to appease them with supernatural tidbits of information.

They have different intelligences, personalities, attributes, and talents, and they will try to express themselves through people.

Those Who Work by Familiar Spirits

Those who work by familiar spirits are called:

+ Enchanters: magicians

- Witches, wizards, clairvoyants: those who practice witch-craft and sorcery
- Mediums: those who consult with familiar spirits
- Necromancers: those who consult the spirits of the dead
- Conjurers: those who summon familiar spirits

> *Then said Saul unto his servants, Seek me a woman that hath a **familiar spirit**, that I may go to her, and inquire of her. And his servants said to him, Behold, there is a woman that hath a familiar spirit at Endor. And Saul disguised himself, and put on other raiment, and he went, and two men with him, and they came to the woman by night: and he said, I pray thee, divine unto me by the familiar spirit, and bring me him up, whom I shall name unto thee....And the king said unto her, Be not afraid: for what sawest thou? And the woman said unto Saul, I saw gods ascending out of the earth. And he said unto her, What form is he of? And she said, An old man cometh up; and he is covered with a mantle. And Saul perceived that it was Samuel, and he stooped with his face to the ground, and bowed himself.*
>
> (1 Samuel 28:7–8, 13–14)

The witch at Endor could bring up Samuel because he was in captivity, awaiting the shed blood of Christ, or the atonement. Notice the Bible did not say the witch brought up an imposter; she brought up Samuel himself. Just as a warden can release any prisoner from the cell as long as he or she is in custody, so a medium can bring forth an evil spirit with satanic power. He or she has can use all the host of hell to deceive and win over people for Satan.

It should be noted that conjurers cannot summon jus-tified spirits, because Jesus has taken them to heaven. (See

Matthew 27:52–53; Hebrews 12:22.) But they can summon evil familiar spirits that may be from the same family and who might know the personality traits of his justified family members. For this reason, these familiar spirits will be assigned to work in their own family, to impersonate others.

Manifestations of Familiar Spirits

Split Personalities

Familiar spirits can cause split personalities. We already know that a person can be possessed by numerous evil spirits, and that each spirit has a personality of its own; so, when there is more than one spirit living in someone, it is not uncommon to see various types of habits, personality traits, appetites, lustful desires, and so on, manifested in his or her life. Hence we see split personalities. When a person is completely over-thrown by spirits, he is subdued, conquered, and suppressed. When he is possessed completely by familiar spirits, we call him "insane."

Insanity

Insanity is the end result of the collaborative work of 1) the spirit of fear, 2) the dumb and deaf spirit, and 3) the familiar spirit.

When the spirit of fear and the deaf and dumb spirit have attacked, wrestled with, and gained control over their victim, they turn him or her over to the familiar spirit. At this point, the three demons have gained control of the person's mind and body, which is capable of horrible acts of violence, both against him- or herself and others.

Schizophrenia

It is possible for a person to be only partially in control of his or her own body and souls, while a familiar spirit shares equal control. Unless they are resisted properly, these spirits will control a person's will. This is a manifestation of schizophrenia.

Schizophrenia is characterized by disassociation from the environment and deterioration of personality, or also what we call "split personalities"—more than one personality in one body. At times, the human spirit is bound, and the familiar spirit uses the body for its purposes, and vice versa.

Science has not yet found satisfactory answers to the two big questions on schizophrenia: what causes it and how it can be cured. But the Bible has given us some wisdom about the mental disease. Yes, Christians who read and understand God's Word by revelation of His Spirit of wisdom can tell you exactly what causes schizophrenia and how it can be cured.

Therefore, schizophrenia should be treated by medical personnel as well as the clergy. A psychiatrist may discover that the cause of a mental sickness is demon related, but if he or she is not filled with the Spirit of God, he or she should not attempt to cast the spirit(s) out. (See Acts 19:13–16.) The psychiatrist is not dealing with flesh and blood but principalities of the air. (See Ephesians 6.) Only those who engage in spiritual warfare by the Spirit of God and the authority of His name can successfully handle demon-related cases. Tranquilizing human spirits only makes them more helpless and weak, unable to resist the enemy.

The Spirit-filled worker can bind the strongman who produces evil fruit, putting him to flight by proper resisting forces. We are not supposed to cast out every demon we notice, going to asylums and working in the flesh. People who do not cast out demons by the direction of the Spirit scatter the truth instead of gather it. (See Matthew 12:30.) They will say to God, "Lord, you know me—I cast out devils in Your name," and He will say, "Depart from Me, I never knew you." (See Matthew 7:21–23).

Our work demands our being led by the Spirit of God, so we can free those who are oppressed by casting out evil spirits, giving them opportunities to repent and choose life and blessings instead of death and curses. After repentance, it is of utmost importance that the person receives the Spirit of God, so that he can stand strong in the power of God, enabling him to further resist evil spirits when they return. Furthermore, he must be filled with the truth. Once he knows the truth, it will set him free and keep him free. We must know it and quote it when evil spirits attack.

More Manifestations

Familiar spirits are responsible for passing down evil traits, diseases, inheritances, and unconfessed sin from one generation to another.

Their assignment is to pass on:

1. Curses

2. Sins of fathers and mothers

3. Unholy traits, habits, and tendencies

4. Sicknesses and diseases

Their assignment in the spirit world is to work within families and to turn family members from the paths of righteousness to the paths of evil, leading to everlasting punishment.

What Scripture Reveals About Familiar Spirits

Regard not them that have familiar spirits.

(Leviticus 19:31)

Do not honor, pay respect to, support, or associate with people who have familiar spirits.

The soul that turneth after such as have familiar spirits, and after wizards, to go a whoring after them, [the Lord] will even set [His] face against that soul, and will cut him off from among his people. (Leviticus 20:6)

Thou shalt not bow down thyself unto them, nor serve them: for I the Lord thy God am a jealous God, visiting the iniquity of the fathers upon the children unto the third and fourth generation of them that hate me. (Deuteronomy 5:9)

A man also or woman that hath a familiar spirit, or that is a wizard, shall surely be put to death: they shall stone them with stones: their blood shall be upon them.

(Leviticus 20:27)

[The Lord told the Israelites,] There shall not be found among you any one that maketh his son or his daughter to pass through the fire, or that useth divination, or an observer of times, or an enchanter, or a witch....For all that do these things are an abomination unto the Lord: and because of these abominations the Lord thy God doth drive them out from before thee. (Deuteronomy 18:10, 12)

Now Samuel was dead, and all Israel had lamented him, and buried him in Ramah, even in his own city. And Saul

had put away those that had familiar spirits, and the wiz-
ards, out of the land.   (1 Samuel 28:3)

We are forbidden to fellowship, or have any contact, with any evil spirits. Both the Old and New Testaments forbid us to give them any place in our lives, other than trying the spirits to see if they are of God, and if they're not, to resist them and cast them out of our ourselves, our family members, or others. (See 1 John 4:1.) These are truly dead, cursed spirits that we do not want to commune with.

FOURTEEN

THE WAY INTO
THE KINGDOM OF GOD

The next two chapters present a comparison of the kingdom of God and the kingdom of Satan to show how Satan tries to imitate God in every way.

Why talk about the kingdom of God before the kingdom of Satan? Because a person can hardly understand evil spirits without first knowing the true order of the spirit world and how each member of it is required to function. It is by understanding God's ordained order that we are able to know truth and discern evil.

"The Way"

The book of Hebrews is a revelation of what Christ's death accomplished—God's complete and final work. We are told that we can enter into the New Jerusalem through Christ. We have access to God in His throne room.

> *Seeing then that we have a great high priest, that is passed into the heavens, Jesus the Son of God, let us hold fast our profession. For we have not an high priest which cannot be touched with the feeling of our infirmities; but was in all points tempted like as we are, yet without sin. Let us therefore come boldly unto the throne of grace, that we may obtain mercy, and find grace to help in time of need.*
>
> (Hebrews 4:14–16)

The new and living "way" is presently invisible but will fulfill man's deepest needs! Furthermore, Isaiah told us about *"the way of holiness"* in the end times:

> *And an highway shall be there, and a way, and it shall be called The way of holiness; the unclean shall not pass over it; but it shall be for those: the wayfaring men, though fools, shall not err therein. No lion shall be there, nor any ravenous beast shall go up thereon, it shall not be found there; but the redeemed shall walk there: and the ransomed of the* LORD *shall return, and come to Zion with songs and everlasting joy upon their heads: they shall obtain joy and gladness, and sorrow and sighing shall flee away.*
>
> (Isaiah 35:8–10)

> *Therefore thy gates shall be open continually; they shall not be shut day nor night.* (Isaiah 60:11)

Zion is the city of the living God, where we may go in spirit until it descends at the close of the ages.

> *He that putteth his trust in me shall possess the land, and shall inherit my holy mountain; and shall say, Cast ye up,*

*cast ye up, prepare the **way**, take up the stumbling block out
of the way of my people. For thus saith the high and lofty One
that inhabiteth eternity, whose name is Holy; I dwell in the
high and holy place, with him also that is of a contrite and
humble spirit, to revive the spirit of the humble, and to revive
the heart of the contrite ones.* (Isaiah 57:13–15)

*The Holy Ghost this signifying, that the **way** into the holiest
of all was not yet made manifest, while as the first tabernacle
was yet standing.* (Hebrews 9:8)

[Paul said,] *But this I confess unto thee, that after the way
which they call heresy, so worship I the God of my fathers,
believing all things which are written in the law and in the
prophets.* (Acts 24:14)

The new and living way Paul preached was the way into the
presence of God. Paul worshiped God by submitting to Him
through the new and living Way—Christ.

*And so, dear brothers, now we may walk right into the very
Holy of Holies, where God is, because of the blood of Jesus.
This is the fresh, new, life-giving **way** which Christ opened
up for us by tearing the curtain—his human body—to let
us into the holy presence of God. And since this great High
Priest of ours rules over God's household, let us go right in to
God himself, with true hearts fully trusting him to receive us
because we have been sprinkled with Christ's blood to make
us clean and because our bodies have been washed with pure
water.* (Hebrews 10:19–22 TLB)

When Jesus Christ gave up his spirit, the veil of the temple
was torn in half, from top to bottom. When it was rent in two,
Jesus opened up the *way* into the Holy of Holies. Now His

blood-washed people approach God. Yes, you and I can walk right boldly into the throne room of God Almighty! This was the new covenant with which God replaced the new.

> *The old agreement didn't even work. If it had, there would have been no need for another to replace it. But God himself found fault with the old one, for he said, "The day will come when I will make a new agreement with the people of Israel and the people of Judah. This new agreement will not be like the old one I gave to their fathers on the day when I took them by the hand to lead them out of the land of Egypt; they did not keep their part in that agreement, so I had to cancel it. But this is the new agreement I will make with the people of Israel, says the Lord."*
>
> (Hebrews 8:7–10 TLB)

So, in studying the book of Hebrews, we find that Jesus opened up the way for us, and we *can* go to Him now.

Who Will Be in Zion?

What should we expect to find when we take this privileged trip? To answer that question, let us look at Hebrews 12:22–24:

> *But ye are come unto mount Sion, and unto the city of the living God, the heavenly Jerusalem, and to an innumerable company of angels, to the general assembly and church of the firstborn, which are written in heaven, and to God the Judge of all, and to the spirits of just men made perfect, and to Jesus the mediator of the new covenant.*

Does this mean we can enter the New Jerusalem now? That's what the Book says. But let's look who will join us in Zion.

The Angels

There will be a whole host of heavenly spirits that we will join in paradise—*"the innumerable company of angels"* (Hebrews 12:22 TLB). Imagine there being so many angels you cannot count them!

The Firstborn

As we keep reading, we see others who will join us. *"The general assembly and church of the firstborn, which are written in heaven"* (verse 23 TLB). Who are the firstborn? All of those who were converted before Jesus's blood was shed, from the Old Testament saints to the thief on the cross. These saints make up part of the multitude Christ saved from Satan when He descended into hell, where all of the just departed spirits were held prior to the atonement. Jesus brought these captives to heaven with Him when He ascended on high. (See Ephesians 4:8–10; Hebrews 2:14–15.)

> *And, behold, the veil of the temple was rent in twain from the top to the bottom; and the earth did quake, and the rocks rent; and the graves were opened; and many bodies of the saints which slept arose, and came out of the graves after his resurrection, and went into the holy city, and appeared unto many.* (Matthew 27:51–5)

Now when Christians die, they no longer go into the lower parts of the earth but ascend to the New Jerusalem.

God

We will also meet *"God the Judge of all"* (Hebrews 12:23) in the New Jerusalem. He is the One to whom Job cried, *"Oh that I knew where I might find him! That I might come even to his seat! I would set my cause in order before him, and fill my mouth with arguments"* (Job 23:3–4 ASV). What Job longed for is our glorious privilege. We may come boldly to God's *"seat"* with confidence that we will not be consumed by His majestic splendor. (See Hebrews 4:16.) May we make our petition known to our great and magnificent Father. Oh, what grace!

He is the center of all reality!

Just Men

God really did create us for fellowship, for He said that *"the spirits of just men made perfect"* are in His heavenly abode. Does this mean your righteous mom, Uncle Frank, and Aunt Jane? Certainly! All of those who have died justified by the blood of Christ will be there. They are not dead but alive forevermore, having obtained eternal life. Mark 12:27 says, "[God] *is not the God of the dead, but the God of the living: ye therefore do greatly err."* Isn't that true? Most of our false thinking is a result of not fully understanding this. When Jesus said, *"Let the dead bury their dead"* (Matthew 8:22), He knew that the just had no dead! They had just taken up residence in the New Jerusalem. The Bible said we would assemble with all the righteous people who have departed. This is the assembly of God!

Jesus

We will sit down with Jesus the mediator, the One who brings reconciliation to all who participate in the new covenant. (See Hebrews 12:24.) Jesus is your representative who negotiates all your throne rights and fulfills the scriptural blessings promised to you. His blood spoke better things than the blood of animals Abel had offered. (See Hebrews 12:24.) He has offered a new and better way, so we can *"walk…in it"* (Isaiah 30:21).

The Ministry of Heavenly Beings

So what do all the inhabitants in heaven do? Surely they don't just sit around all day. Besides the great assembly, the host of heaven, each being in paradise has its own particular assignment to bring about the will of God on earth as it is in heaven. There is much written on the ministry of the angels, as well as the duties of the departed brethren. Let us look at a few biblical accounts. One elder in heaven, a redeemed man, spoke to John:

> *One of the elders saith unto me, Weep not: behold, the Lion of the tribe of Juda, the Root of David, hath prevailed to open the book, and to loose the seven seals thereof.*
> (Revelation 5:5)

Furthermore, a departed brother asked John a question, and John answered him:

> *One of the elders answered, saying unto me, What are these which are arrayed in white robes? and whence came they? And I said unto him, Sir, thou knowest. And he said to me, These are they which came out of great tribulation, and have washed their robes, and made them white in the blood of the Lamb.* (Revelation 7:13–14)

Another heavenly being we read about in Revelation 19:10 told John he was a fellow servant, which proves he was a redeemed man, free to come and go from heaven to earth as he ministered to the needs of saints. He said to John, "*And of thy brethren that have the testimony of Jesus: worship God: for the testimony of Jesus is the spirit of prophecy*" (Revelation 19:10). Only people can have the testimony of Jesus. The designation *"brethren"* usually referred to a person's relative or member of his household, as in the house of Jacob, David, Hur, etc. From this we can deduce that these spirits are ministering within their own families.

Entering into God's Rest

Let us labor therefore to enter into that rest, for we have not a High Priest who is unable to sympathize with our infirmities, but was in all points tempted as we are, yet without sin. (See Hebrews 4:15.) So, "*let us therefore come boldly unto the throne of grace, that we may obtain mercy, and find grace to help in time of need*" (verse 16). This is the secret place of the Lord, and those that find it are "*renewed in knowledge after the image of him that created him*" (Colossians 3:10). For here is hidden "*all the treasures of wisdom and knowledge*" (Colossians 2:3; see verse 9). And we all may come into His very presence through the blood! Now, come with me to my Father's house! Come with me to Mt. Zion, the city of the great King!

> *And the ransomed of the LORD shall return, and come to Zion with songs and everlasting joy upon their heads: they shall obtain joy and gladness, and sorrow and sighing shall flee away.* (Isaiah 35:10)

With what attitude should we enter into His presence? With holy boldness, making a joyful noise. Come before His presence with singing! "*Enter into his gates with thanksgiving, and into his courts with praise: be thankful unto him, and bless His name*" (Psalm 100:4). "*Exalt the LORD our God, and worship at his holy hill*" (Psalm 99:9).

When Isaiah had his tremendous vision in the temple, he must have foreseen what a glorious privilege would be ours to enter into God's presence through the blood of Jesus. He said, "*I saw also the LORD sitting upon a throne, high and lifted up, and his train filled the temple*" (Isaiah 6:1). The seraphim were there crying, "*Holy, holy, holy, is the LORD of hosts: the whole earth is full of his glory*" (verse 3). He went into that vision by faith, just as we come into God's rest by faith. Hebrews 4:11 says, "*Let us labour therefore to enter into that rest, lest any man fall after the same example of unbelief.*" Unbelief will block our entrance into the presence of God.

But, sadly, there are those who refuse to enter God's rest. Let's look at Hebrews 12:25:

> *See that ye refuse not him that speaketh. For if they escaped not who refused him that spake on earth, much more shall not we escape, if we turn away from him that speaketh from heaven.*

This is a warning to those who refuse the blood covenant and who forsake the fellowship of the New Jerusalem. The book of Hebrews is God's complete, full, and effective revelation of the work of His Son Jesus Christ. Those who refuse to enter the kingdom of God must beware.

> *Let us therefore fear, lest, a promise being left us of entering into his rest, any of you should seem to come short of it. For unto us was the gospel preached, as well as unto them: but the word preached did not profit them, not being mixed with faith in them that heard it. For we which have believed do enter into rest.…Seeing therefore it remaineth that some must enter therein, and they to whom it was first preached entered not in because of unbelief.*   (Hebrews 4:1–3, 6)

Sometimes, patient endurance is necessary to obtain the promises of God. (See Hebrews 6:15.) Jeremiah said, "*Thus saith the Lord, Stand ye in the ways, and see, and ask for the old paths, where is the good way, and walk therein, and ye shall find rest for your souls. But they said, We will not walk therein.*"

May all people realize that there is no distance between us and God. We are with God, so that we are not speaking to the top of the ceiling, or to the sky, which cannot hear, but to God whose ear is open to our plea.

So, let us speak boldly with all honesty, for we must worship the Lord in spirit and truth. Though your spirit enters into God's rest, you remain physically on earth. The things you see will be with spiritual eyes. The more faith and trust you have in God's Word, the more awareness you will have of Him. Your experience Him will be more vivid.

How to Enter God's Presence

Before you enter His presence, take a little time to prepare yourself. After all, you take time to dress, wash your face, and brush your hair before you go to church. Even so, ask yourself:

1. Have I forgiven everyone who has trespassed against me, so that God will forgive me?

2. Is there any unconfessed sin in my life? Confess it, repent of it, that you may be washed in the blood that was shed for the remission of sins.

Now submit yourself to God! You cannot effectively resist the devil if you do not know the correct way to submit yourself to God. Pray this prayer of praise:

By sacrificing Your own body, You made this entrance possible. I praise You, Jesus, for opening up a new life-giving way for me. I confess my sins and faults before You now and ask You to blot them out with Your blood, that I may be white as snow, justified in the sight of my Father. I cannot go to God my Father except through You, Jesus. I give You honor and glory for this unspeakable gift. It is only right that Your name be lifted above every other name! Oh, Jesus, my Great High Priest who rules over God's household, I adore You and thank You! You are the greatest of all; the Almighty; the all-knowing, ever-present, immutable God! You are the Creator of the world, the sun, the moon, and man himself. Let everything that has breath praise You, Lord!

Now let your request be made known to God! We know that if He hears us, we have whatever we ask for. (See 1 John 5:15.) He hears the prayers of the righteous. (See Proverbs 15:25.)

So what happens when we go into the Holy of Holies, the New Jerusalem, the city of the living God?

> *In* [the Father's] *presence is fulness of joy; at thy right hand there are pleasures for evermore.* (Psalm 16:11)

This is the magnificent realm of His presence! David foresaw the way into the presence of God. He asked the Lord to hide him under the shadow of His wings and to make him the apple of His eye. (See Psalm 17:8.) He joyously proclaimed,

> *How excellent is thy lovingkindness, O God! therefore the children of men put their trust under the shadow of thy wings. They shall be abundantly satisfied with the fatness of thy house; and thou shalt make them drink of the river of thy pleasures. For with thee is the fountain of life: in thy light shall we see light.* (Psalm 36:7–9)

In the presence of God…

+ Our spirits will be refreshed. (See Acts 3:19.)
+ There will be restoration of all things that have been twisted, perverted, damaged, and worn. (See 2 Corinthians 5:17.)
+ God writes His laws in our hearts and gives us the desire to obey Him. (See Psalm 40:8.)

+ We will see only joy and gladness, for no sorrow may enter His gates. (See Psalm 28:7.)

+ Our faith is strengthened. (See Romans 10:17.)

+ We are cleansed. (See 1 John 1:9.)

+ A right spirit is renewed within us. (See Psalm 51:10.)

+ The joy of our salvation is restored to us. (See Psalm 51:12.)

+ We are set free, for the sons of God who are led by His Spirit and do His will are given glorious liberty. (See Romans 8:21.)

+ We receive instruction, teaching, revelation, answers to our questions, and unlimited knowledge. (See Proverbs 2:6.)

+ We find mercy for ourselves and grace for ourselves and others. (See Hebrews 4:16.)

+ Our strength is renewed. (See Isaiah 40:29–31.)

+ We are enabled to teach transgressors God's ways and lead sinners to repentance. (See Psalm 51:13.)

+ We are empowered to speak and teach the truth. (See Ephesians 4:15.)

If we continually spend time in the presence of God through Christ's blood, we will grow closer to Him. He will know us, and we will know Him. There are people who say they know God but do not know Him as well as they could, for they are not interested enough to read about Him. They are the ones who will say, "Lord, You know me; I have cast out devils in Your name." And He will say, "Depart from Me, you workers of iniquity. I know you not. If you are not working with Me, you are scattering!" (See Matthew 7:22–23; Matthew 12:30.)

God invites you to visit Him as often as you like; if you never get around to it, you neither love Him nor know Him.

"A HAVEN FOR THE WEARY SOUL"

Are you tired of the heat of the battle?
Afflicted on every side?
There is rest for the weary,
A place where the soul can hide.

The unredeemed are talking about soul travel,
Projecting their souls into the cosmos.
But I know a place in the heavens
Where only the righteous can go!

Most are waiting till hereafter
But they could walk right in if they knew
Some may never discover,
But the details are found in Hebrews.

The cross of Calvary finished it.
Let me tell you where it's at.
You take some steps toward repentance
And a bath in a blood-filled vat!

Now walk right in, dear brothers,
Without nary a nod,
For that bath made you eligible
For the holy presence of God!

Now that's *soul travel!*

—*Mary Garrison*

FIFTEEN

THE WAY INTO THE KINGDOM OF SATAN

The greatest and most important work of Satan now among men is running a counterfeit kingdom. He represents a false deity, reign, city, doctrine, worship, gifts, miracles, religion, fasting, etc. He simulates all the attributes, ways, and things of God to deceive mankind.

Just as the Bible sets forth the way in which we should approach God, so the devil sets forth a proper way to approach him. Occult rituals are based on the same premise. Satan desires not only to be *like* God but to *be* God. (See Isaiah 14:14.) Therefore, he tries to imitate God in every way, mimicking every attribute and gift. Because of this, we can know his strategies.

I will endeavor to show you the perverted ways and methods of the adversary, Satan, by comparing his kingdom to the kingdom of God

Keys to Understanding the Kingdom of Darkness

God has established His own city—the New Jerusalem—located in the heavens. It is run by righteous order. Satan's city (see Ephesians 6:12) is run by unrighteous order.

God's order involves the work the Godhead, chief princes, archangels, and so on, who rule different kingdoms, and stretches even to human beings who serve as ministers, consecrated servants, and so on. God's kingdom is composed of all who do His will.

In comparison, Satan's order involves evil angels and rulers of the darkness, as well as mediums, witches, the unjust, and so on, who do the will of Satan.

Humans—both just and the unjust—play a large role and are of utmost importance in both kingdoms.

The Just and Unjust

Those who are just will be given a glorious entrance into the very presence of God through the blood of Jesus. The unjust are given a similar opportunity of entering into the presence of Satan.

God required the blood of a spotless Lamb. Satan requires the blood of evil sacrifices, such as filthy menstrual blood, animal blood, or even human blood. Evil, abominable things are used to obtain Satan's favors—the opposite of what the Lamb of God requires.

According to Hebrews 10:22, the righteous are required to draw near to God with *"a true heart in full assurance of faith, having our hearts sprinkled from an evil conscience, and our bodies washed with pure water."*

1. A true heart: earnest, sincere
2. Full assurance of faith: a positive conviction
3. Hearts sprinkled from an evil conscience: the inner man, or spirit, is sprinkled with the blood of Jesus

On the other hand, the wicked draw near to Satan through the opposite:

1. A false heart: insincere
2. Doubt and unbelief of the truth
3. Hearts full of evil from a seared conscience: the flesh is sprinkled with the blood of an evil sacrifice

The evil practice abominable things, such as lapping blood; frothing from the mouth; and using intestines, snakes, and spit to worship Satan. The unjust people who live such wicked lives have access to the kingdom of Satan through *soul travel*. They can project their spirits as principalities and powers of the air, evil angels, evil princes, common demons, strongman spirits, familiar spirits, and damned souls throughout the ages, whose names are written in Satan's book of death.

Yes, the wicked, through blood sacrifice, transcendental meditation, soul travel, astral projection, etc., may come to the seat of Satan—the unholy of unholies.

Parodies

The sons of God do the will of the Father, God, while the sons of Satan do the will of their father, Satan. Knowing that

Satan desires for himself that which pleases God, he instructs witches to use scriptural principles for his advantage by twisting and perverting them. Seeking to please and appease Satan, they render to Satan the things that God requires of the just. For example, the Lord's Prayer is twisted by the children of Satan, who say, "Our Father, which art in the earth...."

Perverted Words and Prayers

The Word of God spoken by a righteous person, along with his or her desire to do the will of God, avails much good. But the Word of God perverted by an unrighteous person, mixed with evil intentions, and along with the desire to have his or her own way, avails much evil.

In fact, words are useful tools for witches and magicians, who cast curses, hexes, and spells. These words are often handed down from one generation of witches and magicians to another. They believe that their words, mixed with desire and belief, will bring about what they are sent to do—a perversion of the biblical principle "believe and you shall receive." (See Matthew 21:22.).

The prayer of the righteous spoken in faith avails much, for when they speak God's Word in faith, believing and desiring it, God answers their prayers. Jesus said, *"If ye abide in me, and my words abide in you, ye shall ask what ye will, and it shall be done unto you"* (John 15:7). Perverting this principle, witches "pray" for and desire evil, and Satan brings their "prayers" to fruition.

Witches also use something called "concentrated imagination," which involves conceiving mental images of what they wish to come to pass. They will project their thoughts toward a victim, actually conjuring up an evil mental vision of what they desire to happen.

They also try to manipulate a person's will, enslaving a negative, submissive, weak, unstable, unfaithful, person. They constantly strive to deceive people into carrying out their own evil purposes.

Satan also tries to imitate the Holy Spirit, who is sent to guide born-again Christians into all truth and to give them power from on high, by sending a spirit of divination, called a "spirit guide," to empower people to do "divine" acts.

Remember, the key to understanding the kingdom of darkness is to understand the kingdom of God. Satan's kingdom is an exact reversal of God's!

What Is Witchcraft?

Witchcraft is "the use of sorcery or magic" or "communication with the devil or with a familiar [spirit]."[4] Witches use many different strategies, artifices, tricks, and devices to work evil. They choose ways to charm, ensnare, mislead, divert, and overthrow their victim, and they use a number of tools to accomplish it, such as potions, rigmaroles, magic charms, incantations, ceremonies, psychic projections, etc.

What Power Do Mediums Employ?

Mediums, such as psychics and witches, have power. We need to recognize and correctly assess their power, lest we lose battles by underestimating the strength of the enemy. Do not ignore them, hoping they will go away. They intend to inflict more and more harm as the age draws to a close. Only by properly resisting them as the Bible teaches will we make them flee.

The power of mediums consist of all the powers and energies of man and all the satanic power they can summon up (familiar spirits) to please their master, Satan.

---

4. *Merriam Webster's 11th Collegiate Dictionary.*

They are all power hungry. There are no neutral forces in the spirit realm. Behind every flow of power dwells a supernatural being. Spirits can work without a medium, but not as effectively as they can when they dwell and work within a human. God works with or without a man, but He has chosen to work through man.

When a medium does a work of the flesh, such as pronouncing a curse, casting a spell, using charms, or utilizing astral projection, his or her work will succeed until a stronger power supersedes it. (See Luke 11:21–22.) Can you recognize the importance for Christians to know these things and use the power that has been given to them to conquer the works of the enemy? It is not enough to read and memorize Scripture, such as Luke 10:19, we must use it!

Make no mistake about mediums. They are children of the devil—submitted, committed, sold-out servants of Satan—enemies of all righteousness! They stalk their prey with cunning. It is folly to refuse to fight them with all of our strength! Their wills are evil; they are working toward seeing our souls destroyed!

Symptoms of Psychic Attack

The victims of such attacks often feel weary, confused, anxious, distressed, or as if they have lost self-control, having a dull, trancelike, or spaced-out mind. This is often a result of a medium captivating a person's mind and bringing it into subjection, as in hypnotism. Victims of such attacks may be afflicted with loss of income, position, and reputation, or experience pain or a disease.

Some mediums are not inhibited by physical distance, attacking any subject at whatever distance, with a strong will unaffected by the elements. It appears that the measure of mediums' strength depends on how many demon spirits they can summon. Often, witches summon evil familiar spirits to go and bind a victim. Then they command these emissaries to carry out their evil wills.

Christian Unknowingly Employing Evil Power

Christians can employ evil power, such as psychic power, without even knowing it. That's why we need to study and know the Word, to show ourselves as workers approved of God. Then we will not be ashamed, rightly dividing the Word of Truth. (See 2 Timothy 2:15.)

Many Christians do not know the difference between evil prayer and power and godly prayer and power! In Acts 19:18–19, we read, *"Many that believed came, and confessed, and showed their deeds. Many of them also which used curious arts brought their books together, and burned them before all men: and they counted the price of them, and found it fifty thousand pieces of silver."* The early Christians were guilty of employing evil power, and so are Christians today. Evil prayer is a counterfeit of Christian prayer. Those who fool around with satanic power cannot inherit eternal life. (See Galatians 5:20–21.)

What Must We Do?

Unrighteous people are carrying out tremendous and mighty exploits for the kingdom of Satan. Christians should be doing exceeding miracles over and above all that the evil ones are doing, for they can only counterfeit the great works of our God by reversing and twisting His Word! Perhaps that is why the church is not prevailing—some Christians do not even get around to reading the Word of God, much less applying it to their lives. Jesus, Philip, Peter, Paul, and many others achieved miraculous feats for the kingdom of God.

The evil ones are busy using psychic power against the president of the United States, the FBI, and all those who are in authority. I once read an account of an organized group of witches who called themselves a church and declared war on the FBI and the United States government! They actually hacked into secret government files. People, we do not stand a chance against this kind of power without the power of the Holy Spirit! Victims of evil attacks do not know what they are up against. That is why we, the church, need to pray for them, especially those in authority. (See 1 Timothy 2:1–3.)

We can do the works of Jesus!

The Works of Christ

Remember that *every* power must yield to the risen Christ! If we are accused of being demon hunters and chasers, let us live up to it! Let us take up our mighty weapons and stalk the roaring, devouring lion. Why be the hunted when we can be the hunters?

These powerful weapons were given to us for warfare. So, let's offend the enemy, not one another. If the enemy is hunting you, you can be sure he wants to devour you. Here is how we can stand against his schemes:

1. Resist the devil, and he will run from you. (See James 4:7.) But don't stop there. Chase him and launch an all-out, powerful attack on him! Don't be lazy; we must be valiant. Bind Satan's strongmen, destroy their goods, pull down their strongholds, nullify their works, pray for and cleanse their victims, heal the sick, and set the captives free. Employ the works of Jesus that

will remain forever. (See Isaiah 47:12–14.) Engage in the battle or get spewed out of God's mouth for being lukewarm!

2.   Stop fighting your brethren. A house divided against itself cannot stand. (See Matthew 12:25; Mark 3:25.) Band together with your fellow brethren who are fighting the devil. Numbers 32:6–7 says, *"Shall your brethren go to war, and shall ye sit here? And wherefore discourage ye the heart of the children of Israel from going over into the land which the* LORD *hath given them?"*

God has endued His people with far superior powers and abilities than the workers of evil can ever hope to attain. With that power, we are to set the oppressed free, break every yoke, undo every burden, and loose all the wicked bands of satanic forces. (See Isaiah 58:6.) The oppressed will remain in bondage if we do not use our power against them, reversing evil. (See Luke 10:19.) It is our job. God instructs us, and we must obey, using the name of His Son, Jesus. How many people are willing to stand up and fight this war? Those who are bold enough to enlist will be very valuable to God's work!

Yes, the evil ones are seducing and enticing thousands of people. On the other hand, Christians are using their power to do greater works than Jesus did when He walked the earth. (See John 14:12.) They are influencing and meeting the needs of mankind. Yet so many people have already gone to church and found that Christians need more help than they do! Some churchgoers have a form of godliness but deny the power of God. (See 2 Timothy 3:5.)

Do not ignore God's unlimited power, which is necessary to bring in the kingdom of God, but study the Bible, put the principles of Christ into action, and start reaping the results.

Prayers of Freedom from Evil

Prayer for Oneself

I come to You, Lord, as my Deliverer. You know all my problems, all the things that bind, torment, defile, and harass me. I refuse to accept anything from Satan and loose myself from every evil influence, satanic bondage, and every spirit that is not the Spirit of God. I command all such spirits to leave me now. I confess that my body is a temple of the Holy Spirit. I am redeemed, cleansed, justified, and sanctified by the blood of Jesus. Therefore, Satan has no place in me and no power over me, through the blood of Jesus.

Prayer to Break Family Curses

In the name of Jesus Christ, I now renounce, break, and loose myself and all my children from all hereditary demonic holds, psychic powers, bondages, physical or mental illnesses, curses as a result of the sin, transgressions, iniquities, and participation in the occult or psychic phenomena of myself, my parents, or any of my ancestors, as well as those of my spouse's family and ancestors. (Ex-spouse[s], too!) Thank You, Lord, for setting us free.

Prayer to Loose Children from Curses and Spells

In the name of Jesus Christ, I now rebuke, break, and loose myself and my children from any and all evil curses, vexes, spells, hexes, bewitchment, jinxes, psychic powers, witchcraft, or sorcery that have been put upon me or my family from any person(s) or occult source. Thank You, Jesus, for setting us free.

Prayer for Ministry

Devils, witches, and cohorts, I see that you are harassing and embarrassing this ministry, attempting to smear and discredit its members so as to discourage others from receiving its benefits. I am not ignorant of your tricks, wiles, and strategies. I command you now to stop your operations, that all of your psychic commands, incantations, prayers, and desires against this ministry may be turned against you. Retreat and flee in defeat. I command that the mouths of all who spread lies about this ministry would be stopped. The Lord rebuke you and all who help you, in Jesus' name.

SIXTEEN

THE CHART

As mentioned before, understanding the kingdom of Satan depends upon understanding the kingdom of God—His spirit world, creation, righteous order, plan for man and the world, and His final plan for the overthrow of Satan and his kingdom. Knowing the truth about all of this is what makes us coheirs with Christ. It is this truth that frees; it is this truth that overcomes the enemy in every realm and on every level; it is in knowing this truth that we can fully understand all other truths, allowing us to be and work in harmony with God and His heavenly hosts. It is only through the victorious work of the cross—the atonement, the access we have to God—that we can confront and defeat Satan and his hosts, with the keys to the kingdom, binding and loosing!

Every realm, being, and law in the kingdom of God has a satanic substitute in the kingdom of darkness. The following comparison chart of the kingdom of God and the kingdom of Satan is not meant to present a complete picture but to show how Satan tries to imitate God in every way. So, know the ways of God, and you will be able to defeat the enemy with the power of the Holy Spirit!

	The Host of Heaven in the Kingdom of God	The Host of Satan in the Kingdom of Satan
Ruler	God the Father	Satan, the father of lies
Representative	Jesus Christ the Lord	The antichrist, or incarnation of Satan
City	Heaven, or the New Jerusalem	Hell, or Hades
Spiritual Workers	• Archangels, such as Michael and Gabriel, who rule over the planets, nations, cities, countries, and communities • Seraphim and cherubim • Common angels who carry out the orders of God in heaven and on earth • Ministering spirits, or angels, who work within families who love God to carry blessings, earned rewards, and good traits from one generation to another for the purpose of winning people to Christ	• Strongmen demons • Evil angels • Princes over the planets, nations, cities, countries, and communities • Common demons who carry out the orders of Satan in hell and on earth • Familiar spirits whose job is to work within families and carry evil traits, curses, diseases from one generation to another, for the purpose of enslaving people to the devil

Human Workers	The sons of God who do the will of the Father and who use the authority of Jesus' name, Spirit, power, dominion, blood, flesh, strength, Word, likeness, and eternal love • Apostles • Prophets • Evangelists • Pastors • Teachers • Lay ministers • Those who are filled with the Holy Spirit	The sons of Satan, who do the will of the father of lies, and who use the authority of Satan's name, spirit, power, dominion, sacrificial blood, and likeness. And all those who share in Satan's eternal damnation and death: • False apostles • False prophets • False evangelists • False prophets • False teachers • Adepts • Sorcerers • Mediums • Magicians
Animals	All animals who bring God glory by doing what they were created to do	All possessed animals that do not glorify God, because they do not do what they were created to do